Letters from the Country

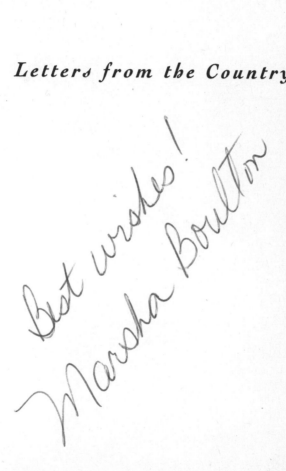

Best wishes!
Marsha Boulton

Letters
from the
Country

by

Marsha Boulton

Little, Brown and Company (Canada) Limited
BOSTON • NEW YORK • TORONTO • LONDON

Second Printing
Copyright © 1995 by Marsha Boulton

Canadian Cataloguing in Publication Data

Boulton, Marsha
    Letters from the country

ISBN 0-316-10375-6

1. Farm Life – Ontario – Anecdotes.   I. Title.

S522.C2B6 1995   630'.9713   C95-930551-3

Cover design: Tania Craan
Cover photos: John Reeves
Interior design and typesetting: Pixel Graphics
Printed and bound in Canada by Best Book Manufacturers Inc.

Little, Brown and Company (Canada) Limited
148 Yorkville Avenue, Toronto, Ontario, Canada

TABLE OF CONTENTS

Summer

Fall

Winter

FOREWORD

WHEN I MOVED to the country 15 years ago, I was approaching 30 and I had spent most of my adult life wearing high heels. As the "People" section editor of Canada's national newsmagazine, *Maclean's*, I interviewed celebritics, actors, writers, musicians, poets and politicians. The scope of my job was such that I was even granted a clothing allowance, since no mortal journalist's salary accommodated the sort of wardrobe that was required to attend everything from embassy parties to film festivals.

In my heyday, I would have scoffed at the notion of trading the chance to have cocktails with Sophia Loren for a barn full of sheep. My childhood love of horses was confined to attending the opening night of the Royal Agricultural Winter Fair and the Queen's Plate. When I watched *Green Acres* on television, I identified with Eva Gabor.

Things change. One day I found myself driving through the southwestern Ontario countryside near the town of Mount Forest with a real estate agent. We stopped. I walked through a huge Victorian farmhouse set on acres of rolling land and woodlot. The next thing I knew, I was signing my name on a dotted line and making mortgage payments. I was in love.

When you think you have found paradise the dream becomes an envelope that seals out reality. I was riding the on-ramp of the Information Highway and a writer's tools are as portable as a modest claret and a ham sandwich. With a keyboard, a fax machine and a modem any village is global. I figured I could live cheaply in the country, grow healthy food, write and make some money raising sheep. I only picked sheep because they looked small enough for me to manage and they don't bite.

You can learn a lot from books, but nothing can really prepare you for farming. I was filled with visions of flowers and trees, newborn foals on wobbly legs, lambs gambolling in the fields and the smell of freshly mown hay. Reality is red ink and rabies and that one little lamb that just doesn't make it. It's sort of the difference between Garrison Keillor and Stephen King or *Lassie* and *Straw Dogs*. Somewhere in between, there is an opportunity to find a balance and a sanity.

For many years, I did not write about my life on the farm. I was too busy making mistakes and learning from them. My neighbours, who populate this book, remain my greatest teachers. Becoming part of their community was the first hurdle I faced.

My farm is forever engrained in the geographic and

cultural mind-set as "the Noonan farm," or more specifically, "the Tommy Noonan farm." Survivors of the Noonan clan are scattered throughout Minto Township, all descendants of Irish pioneers who squatted in the 1850s and finally cleared enough land to be granted title by the Crown. Two hundred acres and two Victorian farmhouses away from mine, stands the still carefully tended Little Ireland graveyard, where the pioneer Noonan, O'Dwyer and Shanahan headstones are aligned as an apostrophe on the past.

Against such a rigid fabric of history, the weaving of a newcomer into the warp is not something that is achieved simply by "buying the farm." Information must be gathered, hardships shared and endured, bowling leagues joined, livestock exhibited, dances attended and euchre hands expertly played.

Indeed, information about each newcomer becomes a commodity that is traded as assiduously as soy bean futures, but with far less attention to detail. Observation and supposition often become accepted as fact. For example, the previous owner of my farm was a distinguished-looking gentleman who only came up from the city on weekends. He had the title of "Dr." before his name. Bearded and bespectacled, in the country he was automatically a "psychiatrist." In fact, he was a biologist.

Word got around fairly quickly that I was a writer trying to farm. I think I was something of a disappointment, because I kept asking basic questions about how to stack hay and what seed to plant in a sheep pasture. I did not speak in iambic pentameter distinguished by

50-cent words. I had no credibility until someone saw my name on a magazine article at the dentist's office.

When I lived in the city, the only neighbour I knew was my landlord. Nobody else spoke, either to each other or about one another. Nobody cared if unread newspapers stacked up outside an apartment door. In the country, if I do not pick up my mail after two days, Len the mailman drives up the lane to make sure I'm still alive.

I take some comfort in that sort of interest.

It took me some time to get used to the fact that when I drive along my concession road, my travel is duly noted by someone along the route. The plain fact is that after 15 years, I know all of my neighbours' vehicles by the sound of their tires. When they drive past the end of my lane, I know the direction they are headed and, probably, where they are going.

If you have a small talent and a willingness to share it, the country will come to you. In 1985, a local committee approached me to help them edit the Minto Township history book. It turned into a three-year labour of love that resulted in a 555-page book featuring more than 700 photographs. *Minto Memories: Families Facts & Fables* became a best-selling book by Canadian standards, but no one outside of the township has ever heard of it. Such is the power of reminiscence.

Through *Facts & Fables* I met the elders of the community and began to understand the spirit of the place where I was laying down roots. Virtually everyone in the community got to know me,since they felt they should. I had all of their family histories in my filing cabinet. Whatever effort I gave, I got back in guidance on everything from ploughing the field so that it "finishes up even" to playing euchre.

Shepherds taught me about sheep, although I did pick up some basic notions from my instructors at the University of Guelph. I spent seven years as the Secretary of the Western Ontario Sheep Producers Association. I learned a lot at those meetings, but even more over the doughnuts and coffee afterward. Animal husbandry is an applied science, and you can learn more about it by spending time in a barn with a knowledgeable farmer than you can from charts and graphs.

I owe a debt of gratitude to the late Alexander "Sandy" Ross, a friend and colleague, for encouraging me to write about my country experience. It was Sandy who suggested to Ian Brown that my country comment might brighten a CBC Radio "drive home" show called *Later the Same Day*. These anecdotal glimpses were written as open letters from the country to anyone who ever wondered what goes on in the environs of a barnyard. A chord was struck because it seems there are countless Canadians who have a farm somewhere in their past or a rural dream somewhere in their future. Ultimately, my "letters" became a syndicated rural newspaper column and I found that farmers got as big a laugh out of following my foibles as city people. For the past few years, I have found a regular broadcast home on CBC Radio's *Fresh Air* program, under the guiding hand of producer Nancy Watson and with the mellifluous tones of host Tom Allen. When those listeners started asking for a book, I dug out my high heels and went to see my publisher, Kim McArthur.

These assembled missives are not a road map to rural life. They are just signposts. I meet people all the time who say they want to do just what I have done but they cannot figure out how.

All I can say is, if you long to live in the country, "do it." Plan for it, but don't plan too long. Life is too short and country roads take too many turns. You may not find paradise, but you'll never know unless you press the edge of the envelope.

— *Marsha Boulton*

ACKNOWLEGDEMENTS

WHEN I WAS a kid I used to visit my Grandmother Fitzgerald on her farm. She would get impatient if I sat in the house for too long.

"Go on out and get the stink blown off you," she would say.

I thank her for her wisdom.

Thanks also to my parents, Marg and Geoff Boulton, who encouraged me to look beyond the boundaries of the suburbia where I was raised.

It is impossible to thank the community of neighbours who have unwittingly contributed to this book. They will find themselves in these pages, even though I have tried to protect some of them with pseudonyms. I hope that the days of tar and feathers are a thing of the past. I have meant no disrespect.

Thanks to the friends and colleagues who have tried to keep my spirits up ever since I told *Maclean's* editor Peter C. Newman that I was leaving a good job, with paid benefits and all prospect of a reasonable pension "to become a shepherd."

I am indebted to that fabulous Toronto restaurant Bistro 990, for providing me with my favourite byline — "Lamb from Marsha Boulton's farm." Many may publish, but few end up on a menu.

My literary representatives at the Westwood-Lord Agency are owed a particular kudo. They promote my work admirably and they also are among my best freezer lamb and capon customers. My publisher, Kim McArthur, shares the same refined taste for the produce of the farm and, thankfully, the stories behind it.

Finally, my heartfelt thanks to Stephen Williams, affectionately known as "Moose-cat."

Spring

Away in a Manger

PREGNANT SHEEP SEEM to think that they
have a lot to complain about. All I hear are grunts and
groans from the time I arrive at the barn in the morning to the last barn rounds before bed. Sheep are not
mean by nature, but they sure get cranky in the home-
stretch to lambing.

I can appreciate that they might have mood swings.
After all, I'm sure I'd be less than perky if I were carrying twins or triplets and looked like an inflated marsh-
mallow ready to burst. The gestation period for sheep
averages out to between 148 and 152 days. The first
100 days are a breeze, but in the last trimester, the
lambs start growing — and growing. My library of
"how to be a shepherd" books yields the useful advice
that as much as 70 percent of the growth of unborn
lambs takes place in the last six weeks. Now that's a
growth spurt.

The ewes seem to expand on a daily basis. Sides
bulge and udders that were barely visible two months

ago swell in preparation for milk production. The sheep do not kick up their heels anymore. They sort of shuffle around. If they are in a hurry, they just shuffle faster.

Ewes that used to listen for my footsteps in the barnyard and line up smartly for their grain are now slow to even bother getting up when they see me. They have not lost their appetites, however. With all of that growing going on, they need extra grain — whole grains only, if you please. I add soya meal for a protein boost and a lick of molasses to make it tasty. This is washed down with so much fresh water that sometimes I swear they should be floating. Ewes with a due date drink four times as much water as usual.

Their hay is only the finest. It should smell as sweet as a summer day and look green enough to take into the house and dress with vinaigrette. Only then is it good enough for my ladies. Since they do not have a lot of room in their four-stage ruminant stomach with all those lambs taking up space, the issue of quality is critical. An old shepherd once told me that he could share his secret of a lifetime with sheep in six words.

"Feed them and feed them well," was all he said.

For all the tender loving care I give, all I get are long lazy sighs. When I scatter their bedding, they lounge uncomfortably looking for all the world as though they expect fluffed pillows instead of simple straw. When they choose to lie down it can take several minutes. First there is the drop to the front knees, followed by a grunt. Then somewhere between gravity and willpower, the hind legs fold and the ewe adjusts the configuration of legs, udder and lambs until she is satisfied.

The demands just never stop. One wants her head scratched; another casts me a baleful glance when I laugh aloud at the antics of a chicken. Some of them enjoy a sliver of apple; others spit it out. There is plenty of attitude. Dominant ewes stake out their territory. They will accept certain of the flock as their neighbours, but nudge away those they do not like. Some ewes snore a bit more loudly than others. Some of them are subject to explosive flatulence.

The older ones know what is going on. They know that this is their time to be pampered. They know that I will forgive every last woolly one of them for being so demanding. Someday soon, I'll be holding a newborn lamb, and that makes all the grunts and groans worthwhile.

Mailbox Murders

Here in the country we still have mailboxes, and on my rural route the mailman, Len, is an expert at deciphering illegible handwriting on envelopes addressed to me. If I put insufficient postage on a letter or parcel, I will often find a note from Len advising me that he paid the extra few cents, and the next day I leave the change in the mailbox for him to pick up. With thanks. Now *that* is service.

You get attached to your mailbox. It becomes a sort of signpost for directions. In blinding rain or snow, the old mailbox is a faithful and familiar marker.

It's a pleasant walk to my mailbox — a kind of Zen stroll with plenty of time to pause and examine the buds on the trees for signs of spring. And around this time of year there is a particular excitement to fetching the mail, because seed orders are arriving. Every box contains wonderful surprises that looked good in the catalogues during a January blizzard.

So when your mailbox is murdered, it's upsetting. It is also a sure sign of spring.

A few days ago, I found my mailbox lying like a slain thing at the side of the road. Mine was not the only mailbox slaughtered in the night. Mailbox murders tend to be cluster killings.

I have had half a dozen mailboxes cut down in the prime of their lives. At first I used to replace them with those cutesy mailboxes with birds on them or the ones that are shaped like barns and cost 50 bucks. But finally I got smart. At local auctions, I stocked up on well-worn mailboxes in need of a coat of paint.

Pretty mailboxes are primo targets. The ones with a few dents and a bit of rust tend to survive longer. I know one retired farmer who spent an entire winter crafting a Chinese pagoda-shaped mailbox out of Popsicle sticks. It lasted for two days and the remains were never found.

I have sort of resigned myself to the concept of losing a mailbox every spring. But when my neighbour Cheryl's mailbox went down, she organized a midnight posse. Now we call her Sheriff Cheryl.

Although mailbox killers generally strike only one area per year, Cheryl was not going to stand for having her new mailbox destroyed. She patrolled the concession half the night waiting for the return of the midnight whackers. And, surprise, return they did.

All we learned for her efforts was that the vandals drove "a big black car with tail fins." Does this mean we have to be on the lookout for Batman and Robin? It would be fairly ridiculous to ask the police to stand guard at rural mailboxes all night long, so I called the cop shop to find out what we could do to protect our mailboxes without becoming vigilantes. The sergeant in charge of mailbox decapitation told me what I already knew — that it happens every spring.

He said great stuff like, "something in the male nature makes them want to do this sort of stuff in the spring — it could be a coming-of-age ritual or a hormone problem. Our civilization has reached the point that they know they cannot pillage and rape so they take out their aggression on mailboxes." So much for the good news.

His most memorable investigation of box bashing occurred when an entire concession of mailboxes was severed and the boxes were all dumped off on the church's front lawn. Only one mailbox on the concession was untouched. "You don't have to be a dumb cop to figure that one out," he advised.

According to the officer, there isn't much anyone can do to protect a defenceless mailbox.

You could build a stone cairn around the post and weld iron bars around the box, but all that does is present a challenge. Hooligans have been known to use their vehicles as battering rams in such cases. One of my neighbours tried installing a battery-operated burglar alarm. It was activated every time the mailbox was opened. This got to be a bit of a pain in the ear, especially for Len the mailman.

The police officer's fantasy solution was to have neighbours organize a sort of group protection plan. In his "to serve and protect" dream, neighbours would link their mailboxes electronically and stock them with small explosive devices. When a mailbox was molested, the electronic device would send a signal to the next mailbox in the chain causing it to blow up approximately 37 seconds later, thereby terrifying the perpetrators. Nice concept.

I applied a rubber mallet to pound out the major dents in my old blue mailbox. Four-inch screws secured it to the post. Then one day I found it crunched on its side with a mortal crease in the metal — another victim of violence. But this time, I took it personally. Inside the scarred remnants of the mailbox, someone had left a funeral parlour advertisement and an empty beer bottle. This was most disconcerting.

The pattern continued and I lost two more well-aged mailboxes to the beer-bottle basher. None of my neighbours suffered similar attacks. I began to spend more and more time checking the box throughout the day, and inspecting the roadway for walkers, bicyclists and slow-moving vehicles. I had a feeling that some cowardly evil was out to get me through my mailbox. Paranoia? Perhaps, but just because you live in a place where it is actually possible to stop and smell the roses, it doesn't mean that you can drop your guard.

My neighbours agreed that the singular nature of the attack on my box and the signature beer bottle was becoming serially suspicious. Cheryl and her husband Jim came up with the solution, courtesy of a piece of two-by-four. They mounted a plastic mailbox on a wooden box that fits neatly over the mailbox post.

Every day, I transport the box to its post before Len

comes, and I pick it up when I know he has delivered. The effect is gives me great pleasure. My mailbox is delivered from an evil that is too gutless to attack in broad daylight. And I enjoy two walks to the mailbox every day, taking time to stop along the way.

MURPHY'S LOBSTERS

I'M THINKING ABOUT putting steel toes on my hip waders when fishing season opens — just in case Murphy is right about the lobsters.

You see, as I was quietly quaffing a cold one next to the pool table at the Mount Royal Hotel and Tavern in Mount Forest, I heard that lobsters are invading our river beds.

It all started with Mike Murphy. Mike is a character you couldn't invent — for some reason we call him Murph the Smurf. When he was a town councillor, he was affectionately known as Mr. Graft. Legend has it that Murph's expenses were right up there with the Mayor's. We're talking a little over $800, including a bottle of white wine he ordered for the table at the Good Roads Convention. That was front page news.

Mount Forest is like a lot of small rural towns. Industry comes and goes. Subdivisions pop up where there once were rolling fields. Local business groups form in order to "put the town on the map." But the local news still runs to police reports that don't name the people who were arrested and social notes about who visited who on the weekend. Hard news can be hard to find.

Still, Murphy has a way of hitting the front page quite frequently. For instance, a few years ago he decided to stop in to see a friend. He happened to be flying a small airplane at the time. When he tried to land it on a ploughed field, there were headlines.

His biggest headlines came when he decided to go over Murphy's Dam in a barrel. The dam is located close to town, and the drop is about ten feet. Murph has a special affection for the dam because it was named after one of his relatives, and he keeps his eye on it.

So one fine day, Murphy went out and had a special steel-rimmed, padded barrel made. He sealed himself in it wearing nothing but a motorcycle helmet for protection.

About 100 people stood on the bridge and watched as Murphy sort of clunked over the dam, landing with a bit of a thud because the water level was kind of low. Murphy was knocked out, but otherwise okay. There were big headlines, and quite a few letters to the editor about the wisdom of allowing town councillors to go over dams in barrels.

That year the town council even considered passing a bylaw restricting the citizenry from going over the dam in barrels. Murphy, however, remains convinced that going over the dam in a barrel could put the town on the map, just like Niagara Falls.

Murphy now works for a local waste disposal company. In a previous incarnation, he says he was a mercenary soldier. In fact, he claims to have been one of two mercenaries who participated in a covert activity some years ago in the Dominican Republic. I seem to have missed that war.

Because Murphy is a great storyteller, it's natural to listen to his tales. Occasionally, he will tell some outlandish story and follow it up with irrefutable evidence. This gives him credibility for another six stories.

Murph was still in my credibility zone when he came into the Mount Royal and announced that the lobsters were running in the Saugeen River. He was cussing and stewing because one of his buddies had just been picked up by the "nature narcs" (conservation officers) for catching lobsters out of season.

According to Murph, lobsters from the East Coast found their way into the St. Lawrence River system many years ago. Gradually, they have been moving into the rivers. They are not monster lobsters because adapting to fresh water has limited their growth to about a pound or a pound and a half. Naturally, he explained, the government was keeping a lid on this because the population was so small and they didn't want any commercial trapping taking place too soon.

Murphy promised to bring me a lobster.

The next day I called the Ministry of Natural Resources. It gave the nature narc on the other end of the line a good laugh. The only new species that had been found in the Saugeen River recently was a lost otter. The biggest crayfish he had seen was five inches long.

While I sat at the pub waiting for Murphy to bring me my lobster, I mentioned the tale to some of the boys. This drew great guffaws, and my gullibility has since become legendary. Apparently Murphy had been telling lobster stories out of school since time began. A lot of mention was made about the stress of the bump on the head he took going over the falls.

"Did he ever tell you about going parachuting when he was a kid?" asked Black Jack the bartender. "He was about seven years old and he got an umbrella and went up to the third floor attic of his house and jumped out the window with the umbrella open."

Everyone except me remembered that one, and great debate ensued over whether Murph had broken one or two legs.

Just then Murphy walked in.

He didn't have my lobster. Instead, he explained that he had not visited his traps at the dam that day because he had been mending his parachute.

A MIDWIFE'S TALE

FOR THE RECORD, there is nothing sweeter than a baby lamb.

Sure a snuffling, oinky, pink baby piglet has a certain charm. And a newborn calf with liquid brown and trusting eyes can melt the hardest heart. But a lamb — now that's something special.

Lambs are snugly. You can hold them like puppies. You can pet them like kittens. If their mother trusts you, they will fall asleep in your arms like a baby.

The heart-tugging beauty of lambs is never more apparent than during that critical period when the shepherd is also a midwife. It is a time of constant watching and worrying. Rounds of the barn must be made every couple of hours — day and night. The effort is wearying, but the result is holding new life. I wouldn't miss it for the world.

A shepherd knows when a ewe is intending to give birth because sheep tend to dig a sort of nest before they have their lambs. It is the oddest thing. The ewe will go off into a corner and begin to paw in one section of the straw, all the while making a guttural baaing sound that seems to come from deep in her chest.

Then the water bags appear.

It scared the living daylights out of me the first time that I saw one of my sheep digging madly in the straw with what looked like a liquid-filled balloon hanging out of her backside. Fearing a crisis was occurring on my first time out of the gate as a sheep midwife, I placed a panic-stricken midnight phone call to an experienced shepherd.

"Did they teach you nothing at that university?" he asked. Then I heard him snicker to his wife: "The girl's so daft that she doesn't even know about water bags." I left the phone red-faced, with instructions to get back to the barn and watch.

That was 15 years and hundreds of births ago, but everything about the process still strikes me with wonder.

Most sheep are quite capable of delivering their lambs all by themselves. All I have to do is daub the lambs' navels with iodine to prevent infection and watch to see that they find the food source. The ewe licks her newborn lambs and prods them to their feet, from whence they toddle in the general direction of the faucet of life.

You can always tell when a lamb has found mother's milk because its tail wiggles like a happy puppy's. That first milk, the colostrum, is crucial to the lamb's survival. It is thick and rich, loaded with vitamin A and protein and all sorts of antibodies to protect the newborn from bacterial infections. When the lamb has figured out the food source and had its fill, I get out my clipboard and attend to the administrative duties of the shepherd. This includes identifying the lamb by placing a numbered metal tag in its ear, noting the sex, the birth weight, the number born and the mother's tattoo number. Once everything is duly noted and going nicely, the lamb family moves into a private pen where they can spend "quality" time getting to know each other for a week or so.

Twins are a common occurrence in sheep and they are the goal of most breeding programs. Triplet lambs are a bonus. I have even had a few sets of quadruplets. Nature is full of surprises.

When I have to help deliver lambs, it is usually a multiple birth. Lambs should ease into life front feet first, but there are always lambs that are determined to be born backwards, sideways or in some odd combination of legs and head. This is hot, soapy water time for the shepherd midwife.

Untangling lambs and repositioning them gets to be up-to-the-elbow-in-sheep-work. It is slow and patient work — gentle work that requires enormous trust between the midwife and the ewe.

In a way, it's like being an intimate Lamaze coach for someone who does not speak your language, but I expect that the ewe can understand from my tone of voice that I'm helping her. We are a team.

Once the first lamb is delivered, the ewe's spirits rise and so do the shepherd's. But there is no time for awe — the lamb's nostrils have to be cleared immediately to ensure that that first breath of life jump-starts the little critter and tells it "yep, I'm born." If the ewe is tired, it's up to the midwife to towel-dry the lamb, stimulating it to stand up and seize the day. A nice bucket of warm water flavoured with molasses can usually perk up the old mom, and a cup of soothing tea does wonders for the shepherd.

Birthing can take hours, or it can be over in a matter of minutes. I have seen older ewes deliver two fine big lambs with natural grace and then stand up and deliver a third one as though they were spitting out a watermelon seed. First-time mothers sometimes fret and panic, but once their lambs are born the mothering instinct takes over. In fact, sometimes a hugely pregnant ewe is so anxious to have a lamb that she just cannot wait for her own to come and tries to steal another newborn away from its mother. In other cases, the act of one ewe giving birth seems to inspire others and the next thing the shepherd knows, the stage is set for a marathon of midwifery. Life is never boring in the sheep maternity ward. I had a five-year-old visitor who summed up the process nicely — "totally awesome."

It doesn't take long for day-old lambs to start butting heads and dancing backward at the sight of their own shadow. Ewes that once needed me will stomp their hooves in protest if I dare intrude into their space.

But every once in a while, I will be allowed to hold a woolly baby and marvel, as we do with all newborn things, at the perfection of little ears, innocent eyes and tiny, tubby tummies. And that's why there is nothing sweeter to me than a baby lamb.

FLY WARS

I GUESS THERE are some questions that just cannot be answered. For example: "Where do all the flies come from?"

As soon as the sun starts to warm my window panes, flies seem to emerge fully grown to crowd onto the window ledge and buzz away at the outside world where they belong. Who are these flies, and why do they think they should live inside my house?

These are not smart flies. They don't even try to fly away when I come at them with the swatter. And swat as I may, an hour later still more dastardly flies will be buzzing away on the ledge.

I make no claims about being a great housekeeper, but I certainly do not deliberately leave fly food lying around my house. Yet the flies are not starving to death. I don't put out a water bowl for them. So why don't they just dry up or leave?

Granted, I do not live in a hermetically sealed environment. Dogs are always begging to go outside and I am always traipsing out to the barn. I can accept that a couple of flies might slip in occasionally, but that does not explain the hordes of flies on the window ledge in the guest bedroom.

I have tried just about every flying insect killer on the market. The most effective types seem to be those that are used in milking parlours, but considering some of the precautions on the labels I've had to think twice. When a product recommends that a space should be ventilated for 30 minutes after spraying before a half-ton cow is allowed back in the room, it makes me wonder how long a person of my body weight has to stay outside.

My grandmother used to hang flypaper in her old farmhouse.

When all the aunts and uncles and nieces and nephews came to visit and the house was bulging at the seams, I'd get to sleep on the kitchen couch next to the woodstove. It was fun, until the morning sun shone through the windows and activated the sleeping flies.

I would wake up to their steady tormented buzzing from the flypaper. I would listen to their little fly screams, and pray for the rooster to start crowing so that everyone would wake up and save me from the chamber of flypaper horrors.

So I will not have flypaper in my house. I tried it in the barn once, but I forgot to tell the banty hen who flew into it while escaping from a dog. Removing flypaper from a frantic chicken is no fun.

I have been told that flies can somehow weasel their way through the smallest gap in old wooden window frames. So I thought about replacing the windows. A friend recently tried this, and I called to find out whether or not it had worked. It hadn't.

The next theory is that flies can weasel their way through old bricks and mortar and underneath shingles. However, the prospect of new windows, new roofing and new walls is utterly unrealistic.

Of course, I could always move. I have a friend who lives in an elegant apartment 21 floors above a busy Toronto intersection. There are no flies up there. The windows do not open. There is no breeze scented with the fresh smell of the earth awakening to a new season. Instead of flies droning, the background sounds consist of sirens and honking horns. Somehow I think putting up with a few flies is a less stressful option.

The fat and furry flies of spring will disappear shortly, to be replaced by the wily and more manageable flies of summer. In the meantime, I will wage war on the many-eyed insects with my faithful vacuum cleaner. I will try not to hear their death buzz as they are sucked into oblivion, and I will show no mercy when I stuff the vacuum nozzle with a rag soaked in bug killer to dissuade any fly escape artists.

In the quiet of the evening, when the lights are out and the flies are dreaming little fly dreams, the spring breeze will rustle through the buds on the lilac bushes. No wonder the flies like it here.

THE RICHEST DOG IN CANADA

ONE NICE THING about being a shepherd is that you are never stuck with providing a boring answer to the ubiquitous urban question "and what do you do?" Most city people have never met a shepherd. Before I became one, I had never met a shepherd. So after the initial shock of hearing something totally different, some form of discussion is bound to ensue. And that is how the richest dog in Canada came to live with me.

I was attending one of those mammoth charity affairs orchestrated by the ladies-who-lunch. The theme of the day seemed to be "the lady with the biggest hat wins." Even the people serving lunch wore doilies in their hair. A girlfriend's mother had cajoled me into doing some writing and fund-raising for what was a very good cause. The "free" lunch was my reward. Hatless, I sat where I was told and tried to blend in with the crowd.

There were seven other women at the table and collectively I would estimate that their hat bill could have made a significant dent in the national deficit. They talked amongst themselves about far-flung vacations and hat-hunting expeditions, until a gracious table-mate turned and asked me the ubiquitous question.

A torrent of queries followed about sheep and what it was like to raise sheep and where one acquires the best lamb chops. When the luncheon ended, I was enthused by the prospect of signing up a few new freezer lamb customers. My girlfriend's mother told me that from her head-table position she thought our group seemed to be having the best time in the room.

"We talked about sheep," I told her.

"Just the thing we need," bubbled my hostess. "Something different."

A few weeks later, one of the women called me at the farm. Her name was Shirley, and I remembered her joking about renting a sheep to trim her lawn. Her husband was newspaper potentate Conrad Black, so I suggested a *bete noir* would be appropriate. But Shirley was not calling to rent a sheep. She wanted to arrange an adoption.

The adoptee was a six-month old Shetland sheepdog, which had been purchased on something of a whim for their children. However, transatlantic travel plans and the general failure of the puppy to adapt to an elite lifestyle had rendered it "a problem." Also, the pup had taken to relieving itself in the master's shoes.

City people often live under the fantastical notion that the kindly farmer always has room for another dog, but so few bother to ask. When they have an unwanted puppy, they drive out into the country and drop the animal off near the end of a laneway for the kindly, anonymous farmer to "find." If it does not wander into traffic, or starve, or become fodder for a hawk, the poor animal is most likely to end up running with other abandoned, wild pets and harassing livestock. Then the kindly farmer ends up having to get out the varmint gun.

If it does not become a dog dumping ground, "the farm" is also often perceived as doggy heaven by people who don't want to live on a farm themselves. I still remember the day my suburban parents told me that our boisterous, wild-hearted mongrel, Bingo, had gone to live on a farm where he could run and be happy. The same six-year-old school chum who shattered the myth of Santa Claus for me told me that Bingo had actually bought the farm on the bumper of a delivery truck. I forgave my parents that betrayal. I still prefer to think Bingo is frisking around a farmyard somewhere.

So when Shirley asked me to take the dog, I recognized her plaintive cry for honourable closure and her good manners.

"One dog's a companion," says the wit and wisdom of my neighbour Elmer. "Two dogs make idiots of each other, and three dogs make an idiot of their owner."

I already had two dogs. Not exactly what you would call "farm dogs," either. My big red bullmastiff, Mingus, lived in terror of sheep after being rammed as a puppy. Diva, the slightly wrinkled Chinese shar-pei, still thought that groundhogs wanted to be her friend.

Idiotically, I thought a bona fide Shetland sheepdog would render some sanity to the kennel.

In a burst of originality, Shirley had named the puppy Sheltie. She was a tricolour bread-box of a dog, with a white mane, a white tip on her tail and a pointy nose. I picked her up at a mansion. Shirley and the butler put her into a dog travelling crate, along with her yellow blanket.

"She's shy and she doesn't like big shoes," Shirley told me.

The little dog stayed in her crate for a solid week. She would only venture out of it when I put it on the porch. Then she would skitter out and do her business before rushing back to the comfort of her blanket. She would only take her food and water in total privacy. The other dogs would peek in the crate at her, but she would not come out and play.

Like people, animals that are thrust into unfamiliar situations need time to adjust. Before I tried to saddle my youngest horse, I spent two years getting her used to the idea of standing to be groomed and picking up her feet to be cleaned and trotting in a circle on a long lead. Cows do not automatically line up to have milking machines fastened to their udders. It is all a matter of routine and trust.

Gradually, Sheltie and I became friends. She liked to be cuddled and stroked and tummy-rubbed, but only when we were alone. No sharing with the other dogs. She would not play with their "toys," and she hid her squeaky toy under her blanket after each session.

Getting her out and about was another thing. She was a dainty dog and the notion of sheep sniffing her did not sit well. Her herding instincts came into play with the goose gaggle. All it took was a touch of praise, and Sheltie took it upon herself to ensure that the geese stayed behind their fence and feared to stray anywhere near the house or the garden.

I grew to love the eccentric, timid creature. Sheltie and shar-pei made great sport of each other, racing around the yard and sniffing out groundhog holes. They made perfect idiots of each other, until exhaustion set in and I would find them snoozing next to the cedars beside a patch of pansies. When the much-loved Mingus met his maker courtesy of a speeding cement truck, Sheltie was a comfort and she seemed to understand my pain.

As sensitive as she was to me, Sheltie had little concern for others. She had a most irritating bark that she would let rip with when anyone came to visit. The only way to shut her up was to confine her to the crate, where she huddled quietly, waiting for the intruders to go away. Any male guests with big shoes had to tread lightly around her. She could urinate on a shoe faster than any dog I have ever seen.

I met the Blacks at a Christmas party one year, and they inquired after Sheltie. I sensed they had felt a certain failure with the puppy, and there was some relief in knowing that she had indeed found happiness.

Privately, their young son came to me and asked if Sheltie was *really* living on my farm. It took me back to my childhood and the times when I had wanted to confront my own parents about the true whereabouts of poor Bingo, but never had. It was great to look a little boy in the eye and tell him, "Yes, your puppy is on a farm and she's having the time of her life."

Just Say No to Porcupines

DRUGS ARE SERIOUS business. Addiction is serious business. But somehow I never expected that any of the animals on my farm would develop a "habit."

The truth is that one of my horses seems to have a craving for tranquilizers.

Her name is Karma. She is a half-thoroughbred, four-year-old golden palomino, and she is the first horse I have raised from a foal.

She was born just outside my living room window. Her mother, Lady, was let loose in the yard before she foaled because she seemed to want to be close to me. She liked to look through the window and watch TV.

I had the vet on call for the birth. Neighbours who raise horses were quizzed thoroughly about equine midwifery procedures and birthing complications. Ultimately, one June morning there was a little horse running around the garden with Lady.

Karma was a wondrous spindly-legged thing. Once she had figured out her food source and gotten her footing, she rested. I found her lying flat out amid a patch of purple lupins, resting in the morning sun while her mother grazed nonchalantly nearby. At first, I breathed softly in her nostrils. Then I rubbed her all over from her ears to her tail. We have been good friends ever since.

It's hard for me to accept her as a drug addict. She only seems to get the craving in June, but it has happened every year for the past four years. I think we can safely say an unhealthy pattern is emerging.

Karma gets her drugs by sniffing porcupines.

She had her first taste of tranquilizers when she was a yearling and decided to investigate a spiny woodland creature. Unfortunately, she used her nose.

Now you can't just tell a horse to stand still while you get out the pliers and pull the porcupine quills. The vet suggested we sedate Karma for the duration, and the drugs took effect pretty fast. First Karma's lower lip became loose and quivery. Then her ears slopped off both sides of her head like a pack mule. Her eyelids drooped like Tammy Faye Bakker's on a bad day, and her long white tail folded like a mop between her legs.

When her front knees bowed, the vet and I helped crumple her to the ground, where she stretched out and began to snore.

I whispered comforting thoughts to her about carrots and apples, while the vet snipped and plucked. The whole process took about an hour, by which time

Karma was ready to rejoin the land of the living but was far from "straight." In fact, she spent the next quill-less 48 hours hobbling around staring at fence posts and contemplating blades of grass like a refugee from a party at Timothy Leary's.

Altogether, the horse was a model of mellow.

The first time it happened I could accept her porcupine nuzzling as a mistake made out of curiosity. The second time, I accepted it as the error of a half-ton animal fueled by a two-pound brain. But since it has happened regularly every June for the past four years, I'm beginning to see it as a larger problem.

Fact is, I swear she sniffs porcupines because she knows that, for all the aggravation they cause her, she gets drugs that make her feel a weirdness she can't get from straight oats and hay.

Perhaps it is time I had a Betty Ford-style confrontation with Karma and the porcupine family. Or maybe I should just call out a porcupine posse and lock Karma up in the orchard for a year or two.

There aren't any "say no" brochures about dealing with four-legged tranquilizer addicts who only strike in June with porcupine accomplices. I guess I'll have to try "tough love" while Karma goes cold turkey next June.

THE MOTHER GOOSE WARS

GEESE KNOW NO mistress.

At the best of times, they are bound to peck the hand that feeds them. In the spring, when they begin laying their eggs and tending their nests, they become commandos and straying too close sets off the mother of all goose wars.

Geese in a defensive mode are not attractive. Their necks crane and flatten out like feathered vipers. They wave their heads, weaving from side to side in a goosey rendition of the evil eye. One step too close can elicit a hissing volley. It is a long expulsion of goose breath that is made even more intimidating by the waggling of their dreaded goose tongues, which are peppered with spiked ridges. When they feel threatened, they attack with their wings spread and peck at any appendage within the grasp of their hardened beaks.

My geese are of the Toulouse variety. They are big grey birds about as tall as a regulation-sized three-year-old. A group of geese form a gaggle, and that is about what they sound like as they waddle around honking and yakking away to each other.

I have heard that the Chinese once kept geese to ward off intruders and it certainly seems possible. Mine function as barnyard doorbells. Any vehicle that ventures up the lane is heralded with honks and hisses from the goose collective.

You can say "goose" to just about anyone who grew up on a farm and a tale will unravel about an old gander that loved to torment children with hissing flights of fancy and toe-pecking antics. The fact is, my buddy Loggie contends he would have never made it beyond the third grade if it had not been for the old grey goose chasing him down the lane and onto the school bus.

My unruly gaggle are the descendants of a trio who escaped the annual harvest five years ago. They were just too fast and feisty for me to capture. They have been multiplying ever since.

Goose mating is an awfully noisy, rambunctious affair. They mate in freezing rain. They mate in snowstorms. They mate at dawn or in the afternoon. But usually they mate around midnight.

From all of the honking and hissing and running around they do, I don't think you would call this activity an act committed out of love. At first, I thought they were just trying to keep warm. Unfortunately, they make the same sort of commotion when a fox ventures too close. It has caused me to make a rush to the barnyard more than once.

And there I'd find them, coy as teenagers caught

necking on a sofa. Some calmly smoothing their feathers and others swaying their necks. They would even honk at me as if to say "Yeah so nothing's happening here, lady. What's the beef. Chill out."

They have a goose house, but they prefer to winter in the snowbanks along the fence line where they can keep an eye on me. In their purely belligerent and self-reliant tradition, they totally ignore the nesting boxes I built for them. This year, four of them are nesting on top of the manure pile. Two are cleverly hiding out in the straw loft and the rest have planted their nests squarely in the middle of the barnyard gateway. One young goose is so befuddled by this egg-laying business that she simply deposits them in the middle of the laneway and runs away.

A nest of eggs is called a clutch. Being clutched by a goose is what you risk when you try removing eggs. Early in the spring, I gambled my digits to gather fresh eggs that would have otherwise suffered from frost damage. One goose egg makes a fine omelette and I had a couple of double-yolk goose eggs that scrambled into brunch for four.

The geese have been sitting on their nests for weeks now. Every few hours they go through a strange ritual of examining their eggs and rolling them around with their beaks and their feet to ensure an even and constant heat. The nests are lined with downy feathers that they have plucked from their own breasts. When they take an occasional stroll, the eggs are prudently covered with down and straw.

As I wander around checking on lambs and repairing fences, I can hear the constant, low-level, one-way chattering they maintain with their eggs. I imagine them saying: "Never trust the blond human. Always hiss at her and bite her if you can." Those would seem to be typical goose training instructions.

When the first gosling hatches, it triggers a maternal frenzy of honking and fretting and rolling of eggs. Such a fuss over an awkward ball of fluff with tiny orange webbed feet that are the buttery texture of fine suede.

Inevitably, one over-anxious goose will abandon her own nest to sit next to the real mother, who hides the gosling under her wings and pecks angrily at the intruder.

I checked with my neighbour, Scotty, who has been raising web-footed creatures ever since he gave up truck driving many years ago, and apparently the phenomenon of abandoning a nest in favour of surrogate motherhood is not uncommon. There is no ready fix. Other less fickle geese will adopt the abandoned eggs, although placing them in new nests may require the protection of welding gloves and a construction helmet.

Once all of the goslings have hatched, the geese will lead their flopping and stumbling babies to the pond. Great displays of honking and flapping will defend them from curious lambs and warn the wild ducks to keep their distance.

Soon the goslings will be cruising the water, practising their goose-breath hissing at the frogs and giving the evil eye to the turtles.

I guess there are some things you have to be a Mother Goose to love.

HOLD THE KITTY LITTER — THE CAT CAME BACK

YOU REALLY HAVE to hand it to my old cat Webster. He's 12 years old and still purring like a kitten, even though he has surely used up more than his share of the proverbial nine lives.

Webster is a barn cat. He started out life living in town, but when he decided to make a habit of destroying curtains and toppling knick-knacks while his owners were at work, he came to live with me.

The sheep loved him instantly. He is pure black, and when the ewes first saw him they assumed he was a lamb. He lives with them now. Sometimes he even sleeps on top of one of the old girls.

Barn cats have to work for their keep. Webster gets his scoop of feed and minds his business. He hunts constantly, patiently and methodically and since I do not see many mice, he must be doing a good job. Webster has even been known to hunt rabbits and young groundhogs.

When he rubs up against your leg and purrs, it is hard to imagine that he has the heart of a killer. Although his tom-catting career was surgically ended many years ago, Webster has an uncanny knack for getting into brawls — usually with species other than cats. He has been pecked by geese, sprayed by skunks, butted by lambs and chased by foals. His early penchant for rubbing against other creatures resulted in a crook at the end of his tail, caused by a calf kick.

Today he doesn't have much of a tail. One winter he decided to abandon his straw bed in the barn and snuggle up under the hood of the pick-up truck. He has always been a sound sleeper, so I guess he slept right through the usual morning commotion of barking and baaing and crowing. When I started the truck, the fan belt devoured all but two inches of his tail.

Webster has never had much luck with vehicles.

At last count, he had been struck or rolled over four times. Nothing serious has happened to him, and he tends to hide himself away while his bruises mend, only to emerge with a slightly tilted gait.

He disappeared for almost a month after being shot clear through by an arrow. Apparently, some young fool had spotted the Web hunting in a pasture and decided to take aim with a practice arrow on what would be considered "an impossible shot."

It seems anything is possible where Webster is concerned, however, and the flimsy projectile whipped right through him, much to the surprise of the errant Robin Hood. Webster ambled up the laneway with the arrow still in him and stood on the front porch looking mildly confused.

I immediately went into paramedic paroxysms. When he saw me coming for him with the traditional blanket used to contain him on trips to the veterinarian, Webster loped off into the bush, with the arrow intact.

I could not track him and, of course, assumed the worst after a few days. Almost a month later, the cat came back — without the arrow. The entry and exit arrow marks were fully healed and Webster was looking for a dish of milk.

Webster has developed a measured dignity over the years. Even the dogs tend to respect his position as senior statesman in the barnyard. Although he still hunts, he has learned to be discriminating. The other day I found him snoozing on a bale of straw just above a banty hen who had just hatched 10 peeping chicks. Webster paid them no mind whatsoever.

Occasionally, I will find him looking weary. But just as I prepare to think about making up a bed for him in the house and tending him indoors during his twilight years, he will roll over on his back purring and then snap to attention, careering across the yard to chase some vagabond chipmunk up the old maple tree.

Webbie's place is in the barn, or stalking the evening pastures or sitting on a fence post in the moonlight. He is not a kitty litter kind of guy, and he never will be as long as he has one life left in him.

RABIES AND RELATIONSHIPS

I GUESS IT might be difficult for a city person to understand the relationship between rabies, travelling salesmen and Jehovah's Witnesses. In the country, I live with all these scourges and in my experience they share a curious bond.

I had a case of rabies on the farm a few years ago, and frankly, I'd prefer to see a Fullarbrush man any day.

One of my cows, Lindy the Limousin, was just not looking right when she should have been starting to look quite pregnant. I put Lindy into a private pen and watched her closely. At first, I thought the isolation made her lonely because she started mooing constantly and pacing like a restless child on a rainy day.

She would not eat grain, even when I tried feeding her by hand. I brushed her and gave her the cow equivalent of a massage. I talked to her and took her temperature. Nothing was working and Lindy was running a bit of a fever. By the time the vet arrived the following day, it was evident that something was very wrong with

Lindy. She was behaving like an animal possessed. Tossing her horns around wildly and charging at the wall of the barn like a Hemingway nightmare.

She was not the cow I knew lying peacefully under an apple tree, snoring as only a cow can and waking only when an apple knocked her on the head. She was a demon. The federal government descended after the vet pronounced the dreaded word "rabies."

Lindy had to be destroyed. Henry the Chicken Farmer, from whom I had purchased Lindy as a calf, arrived in his big diesel four-by-four with a .30.06 calibre rifle. He felled her with one bullet. Any innocence I had left went when Lindy went down. My neighbour buried her with his back hoe and the government took her brain away for analysis. The horror of it sank in and I cried on the slush and mud grave of my beautiful cow.

Of course, I had to have rabies shots. Rabies is a terrifying disease which spreads through the saliva of infected animals, and I'd been thrusting my battered and chafed farm hands under Lindy's drizzling muzzle trying to get her to eat. The shots weren't bad. Five in the arm and I was virtually guaranteed not to froth at the mouth. However, as the news spread through the neighbourhood, I had to endure story after story about the days not so long ago when rabies shots were given in the stomach and the cure was often as deadly as the disease. A few old-timers even recalled the days before the vaccine when a person stricken with rabies was simply led off into the woods, tied to a tree and left to die in screaming insanity.

It got fairly depressing.

My farm was quarantined for 90 days. The dog had to be tied up even though he had been vaccinated. It turned into three months of fear, because the federal vet warned me that, if any other animal on the farm developed symptoms, I could be forced to destroy the whole works. When a horse so much as yawned, I worried.

In its own way, however, there was a lot of peace in those three months. Almost no one came to visit. City friends had no desire to visit a "rabid farm" and even my neighbours were reluctant to drop over for a cup of tea.

The only people who did drop by unannounced and uninvited were travelling salesmen and Jehovah's Witnesses, both of whom seem to share a mission that glues them to a doorstep and translates polite words like "no thanks, I already have some" into an invitation for further discussion. After a few undesired interruptions to refuse pamphlets, cleaning agents, subscriptions and salvation, I remembered the rabies.

I've been using it for years now and it works like a charm.

I greet the uninvited with a cheerful, welcoming smile. Then, just as they prepare to step inside, I feel obliged to inform them that the farm is under quarantine for rabies. The effect is quite dramatic. They vanish. And I bless poor Lindy as they hightail it down the lane.

TIGGER, TIGGER, BURNING BRIGHT...

HOW DO YOU tell a baby lamb that his mother does not love him? It is not because he is stupid, or ugly or poorly tempered. It is not because his high-pitched baa wakes the roosters in the dead of night. Neither his small size, nor his silly habit of hopping in the air and landing squarely on four hooves has anything to do with motherly rejection. So, how do you tell a lamb that his mother just has no love to give him?

The problem is that you cannot explain anything to a feisty, hungry lamb that does not know anything about life, let alone love. You just have to find it a new mother, or become one yourself.

I sat in wonder while a big old ewe I call Wilma delivered her lambs. She was huge and I was expecting a big set of twins or triplets from her. Sure enough, the first two lambs were a healthy size. They were on their feet looking for milk when Wilma sank down again and produced a triplet. I watched and put down some more bedding.

The biggest of the lambs was suckling when Wilma rolled her eyes and plunked her behind down like a sitting dog. She arched back, pointed her nose to the sky and I could see there was another lamb coming! I jumped into the pen just in time to towel off its head, clear its mouth and wipe its little nose. Wilma just looked at it and turned her attention to the trio that were sucking impatiently on her droopy ears.

The fourth lamb was much smaller. While the others tipped the scales at a meaningful nine or 10 pounds, the little guy was half their size. Curled up, you could fit him in a catcher's mitt. He was thirsty from the start, and he wasted no time finding his way to the faucet of life. Poor old Wilma was just beginning to realize the dimension of her production. By the time all of the lambs had enjoyed that crucial first supper, the line-up started forming again.

I guess that's when Wilma put her foot down.

She has always been a good and gracious mother, but her patience (and apparently her reservoir) stopped at three lambs. So every time the little guy tried to belly up to the bar, she butted him away with her nose. He was determined. That is how he earned his nickname, "Tigger."

I suspected this was going to happen. All morning I kept waiting for another ewe to go into labour. If that happened, I could rush Tigger to her side and begin adoption proceedings. Sheep identify their lambs by smell rather than sight. So, in theory, I could rub Tig next to a fresh-born lamb to help him take on its peculiar scent. And I always keep a jug of Royal Copenhagen men's cologne in my medicine chest. Rubbing that olfactory nightmare on a ewe's nose and dousing all of her lambs with it leaves her totally at a loss to sort the poseur from the progeny.

The perfect candidate for foster motherhood was a young ewe who was not overtly tubby. I thought she might have a single lamb and cleave to the tiny Tigger without any problems. Wrong. She had triplets. Of course, by this time I had doused her nose and the lamb with Royal Copenhagen. I sat Tigger down beside me on a bale of straw where we could contemplate the meaning of life and formulate a new game plan. It's hard to think clearly when you smell like a Danish pimp.

The bottle is always my last resort — the one with the lamb nipple, I mean. Tigger was ready to try anything. Nothing is as good as mother's milk, but powdered commercial preparations with names such as "Lambmo" are potable substitutes. Tigger was soon packing back a warm one every few hours. His birth mother allowed him to sleep with his siblings, but an undrawn line remained between him and her precious udder.

Bottle lambs are precious and precocious. Every shepherd should have one because it makes you truly appreciate the value of a good milk-producing ewe. From the moment the lamb tastes milk through that plastic nipple, it is imprinted. The bottle is "king" and the bottle holder is "mother." The first time around this is an endearing experience, but after tending a few bottle lambs it becomes an all too time-consuming experience and an exercise of last resort.

Normal lambs do not socialize with the shepherd. They live in their own woolen world and consort with each other. A bottle-fed lamb, however, is like a demanding child. If Tigger did not get his bottle as soon as I entered the barn, he would let out a cry that could crack an egg. If he wanted more, he would suck at my kneecaps while I was trying to feed and water the rest of the barn. He quickly mastered the art of escaping from any enclosure and thought nothing of toddling along with me and the dogs to fetch the mail. He found a hole in the barn wall that the cats used as an access route and he started showing up on the front porch to cadge more milk. Or maybe just to see what "mom" was up to. He liked to have his chin rubbed, and he liked to be held and burped.

Shepherds are susceptible to projecting themselves onto their bottle babies. Psychiatrists could probably come up with some fancy "syndrome" for it. A woman friend of mine was so touched by her orphan lamb that she took it into her home. Darling little Cricket would wake her in bed each day by bouncing on her pillow. Darling little Cricket was subjected to paper training. Cricket took over the passenger seat of the pick-up truck and on long journeys they made regular pit-stops for bottles and other Cricket business. Cricket on a leash was a model of good behaviour. Her "mother" went so far as to enter the spoiled "baby" in an amateur dog obedience class. To the chagrin of the fourth place Beagle, Cricket took third prize.

By the time my Tigger reached 30 pounds, he was too big to be jumping on my lap, and he was beyond the stage of needing a burp. His bottle grew at the same rate that he did, and soon he was sucking it dry from a holder on the wall. I started catching him poking his head into the hay and discovering the joys of solid food. When I stopped bringing bottles altogether, he pushed me around like a ruffled teenager, and he gave his best shriekish baa. Two weeks later, he was not even interested in a chin rub.

The problem with lambs is that they grow into sheep. Love cannot conquer all.

Shear Delight

I HAVE BATHED four times. I have shampooed my hair six times. My skin is anointed with French perfume and my hands are softer than a Bay Street lawyer's. But I still smell a bit like a sheep.

Yesterday we sheared the flock. For hours and hours I was tackling wool on the hoof, trimming sheep feet and tying fleeces into puffy packages for the market. It is dirty work, and this year it was even more difficult because the ewes are hugely pregnant. Stripped of their wool they look as though they've swallowed bowling balls.

My shearer, Judy, is a five-foot dynamo and she loves sheep. Judy would like to be reincarnated as a sheep. She raises sheep, her brother raises sheep and her father raised sheep. She married a cattle man. Now he raises sheep too.

You can tell Judy has generations of shepherding in her background because she calls ewes "Yos," which is the old-time way of talking about sheep.

Judy hauls her shearing stuff around in the back of a pick-up truck that serves many purposes. When she goes to sheep shows, Judy will often take the sheep she's showing in the truck, along with her shears and grooming stand, a few bales of hay and her sleeping bag. Her truck becomes a sort of combination barnyard motel and beauty parlour.

When Judy arrived, I had all of the ewes penned in the barn ready for the first de-fleecing. Unfortunately, sheep don't just line up quietly to be sheared. They have to be caught, wrestled to the ground and set into an upright seated position for Judy to do her work.

After a certain number of years, I have developed a technique that I find works better than my first few shearing adventures, which featured a lot of flying through the air and missing the sheep.

I set my sights on one sheep in the bunch and move slowly toward her. No distraction can deter me once I have set my goal. This is an old trick I learned by watching sheep dogs.

Talking softly, moving slowly with my beady eyes on the chosen sheep, I get close enough to grapple her under the chin with one hand and grab her stubby tail with the other. This can get messy.

With the front and back of the sheep in my control, I can sometimes propel the sheep to the shearing area, but most often the sheep drags me around for a while until we end up there by luck.

Sheep cannot be trained to lie down, roll over and sit up. "Tipping the ewe" as it is called, involves a number of techniques which are prevalent at Wrestlemania events. For instance, if you twist the ewe's head in the direction you want her to fall she inevitably will. But that neck wrenching stuff makes me feel like an unlicensed chiropractor and I cannot bear the bone-cracking nature of it.

You can also try tripping the sheep, but this is tricky because a sheep has four feet while the tripper only has two feet.

This year, Judy and I performed a team effort. Both of us stood on one side of the sheep and we co-ordi-nated our efforts to grab one opposite leg and gently roll the sheep over in consideration of their delicate condition.

Thus prone, I propped the ewes into a sitting posi-tion for Judy to shear.

Judy shears in great long curves down the sides and back of the sheep, trimming around the sheep's cheeks and neck with great delicacy. It is a real art. When she is done, the bald ewe scampers off and the whole fleece lies in one piece on the shearing tarpaulin.

My sheep are Suffolks — the black-faced models. Their wool is not the finest. I think it ends up being used in carpets. Each ewe produces six to eight pounds of wool, and after shearing costs I figure that I earn about 20 cents per sheep in wool sales.

You really have to be a few bricks short of a load to be a shepherd.

The fleeces are bundled and wrapped with twine. It's not like folding a sheet because, of course, each fleece is shaped like a flattened-out sheep. The belly wool is tucked into the middle and the leg wool is tucked under that and then you make four folds to get it sort of rounded out and tie it up like a present.

The joy of folding fleece is in the touch. Sheep produce lanolin in their wool. The stuff you pay for in fancy skin creams oozes from the fresh-sheared wool. It stinks like a sheep, however, when you handle it from the source.

Bruised, battered and desperately in need of a lower back massage, I bade Judy goodbye as she charged off to denude her next flock.

Before the first of many bouts with bubble bath, I went to the barn to check on the girls and assure them that this enforced air conditioning of their bodies was in their best interest.

In the far corner, I found two future candidates for shearing — newborn twin lambs on wobbly legs, nursing at their mother's side. Never was bald so beautiful to me.

LET'S GET READY TO GAMBOL

THE ANNUAL RITUAL of letting the sheep out to pasture has begun.

When I opened the barnyard gate the ewes rushed forward in delight. They have been begging for green pastures since the first sprigs of clover began fluttering in the breeze.

The lambs followed their mothers in a clump. Timorous at first, they were wary of the larger world outside of the barn. Then one bold little ram took a charge across the pasture before stopping dead to look around. The others followed him, just like little sheep, and soon the whole lamb crop was a gamboling mass.

Lambs do gambol. It is the perfect word to describe the dancing kind of gallop-cum-foxtrot that they perform when they are playful. Sometimes you would swear they had springs on their tiny hooves because they tend to bounce in leaps and bounds.

After nibbling at sweet grass and poking their noses around in a sand-pile created by groundhogs, the lambs set about determining the perimeters of their grand new environment.

This is where good fencing comes into play. On my farm, the first pasture new lambs find themselves in is one bounded in part by several strands of sturdy electrified wire. It is something no one can prepare them to avoid, and their discovery of it is always — well — quite shocking.

The great Canadian thinker Marshall McLuhan determined that "The medium is the message." Although he was defining the impact of electronic communication in the Global Village, his vision certainly applies concretely to the true nature of electric fencing.

Sheep can be quite stupid about many things, but when it comes to recognizing the consequences of breaching a charged fence wire, they quickly become mental giants with awesome retentive power.

I have had cattle who would not think twice about trying to go through a brick wall just to get to the other side, but they would halt warily at the sight of a single silver strand of wire. One particularly belligerent Hereford cow, who seemed to feel that going through fences was her purpose in life, met her match when she touched her nose to a wire and found herself doing a bovine tango that would have made any Brazilian dance company proud.

On a personal level, I can tell you that I learned how to break dance, slam dance and fandango simultaneously the first time I "tested" the fence by mistake. The voltage is not strong enough to do any damage, but the shock is definitely enough to create an indelible impression.

I could set a bowl of barbecued hamburgers just inside the electric fence and my dogs might drool and fuss, but they would not be led into temptation. Such is the power of shock therapy.

Electric fencing has been a boon to me because it is lightweight and easy to use for temporary pasture divisions. A single strand of it strategically placed on permanent wire fences and old cedar rail fences helps to prevent the animals from straining their heads over or through the fences.

Years ago, I installed a strand of electric wire above a page wire fence, but I never did get around to hooking it up to a power source. Today, that fence remains pristine simply because the animals have not been willing to bet on what is a live wire and what is not.

Nothing is infallible when it comes to sheep and fencing, but for the time being the borders appear to be secure.

The lambs are contentedly grazing with their mothers. When they tire of eating they form little play groups and tear around the field at full tilt, pulling up to a skidding stop at the fence line. Month-old ram lambs square off to butt heads together and aggressive ewe lambs bully their younger sisters. On a mound of old hay they play king-of-the-castle, galloping to the top and awaiting challengers.

The real gamboling has just begun. Even the old ewes are prone to kick up their heels now and then from the pure pleasure of being in the wide open spaces. From my kitchen window, I can watch the band of lambs chasing killdeers and dancing backwards as puffs of wind blow the heads off a few dandelions.

When the sun is shining and the grass is lush, a shepherd can savour the moment. There really is restorative power in knowing that your flock can lie down in green pastures.

Summer

THE PICKLE SUMMER

THERE IS AN unwritten rule that when an urban person buys a quantity of land, they are bound to make a fool of themselves on at least one acre. The rest of the land may be well-planned for crops, or grazing, or tree-growing. It may be rented to a neighbour who knows what to do with the land. However, there is always that one little plot that seems to cry out willfully: "Do something crazy with me. Boldly go beyond where any normal farmer would dare."

So it is that virtually every urban-transplant farmer that I know has at least one horror story about a wayward experiment in trying to grow anything from asparagus to ginseng. Most often, these failures end up costing money, rather than making it. Most often, they are fuelled by an ambition to get rich quick.

In my case, it started with a little ad in a local paper. Something to the effect that you could earn up to $2,000 an acre growing pickle cucumbers. That sounded mighty fine to me. It was my first year on the farm and

I was determined to make some money. A two-and-a-half acre field just behind the garden looked ripe for cash-crop pickling.

What I discovered is that you don't just grow the pickles, you also pick them and deliver them. And unless you are equipped with a pickle seeder on a tractor, you plant them by hand. I had a neighbour spread the field with sheep manure. It is rich in the nitrogen that pickle plants crave. It was ploughed and tilled and ready for planting.

Armed with my pickle grower's contract and $120 worth of pickle seed, I set out with hoe in hand to plant the rows. On weekends I had two helpers, a five-year-old and a nine-year-old. We planted from dawn till dusk. When you're planting a seed every four inches, two-and-a-half acres seems forever.

"I guess this must be what the slaves felt like," the nine-year-old commented during a mid-row break. The sun beat down and wind whipped dirt in our faces. When we were finished planting I bought the kids bicycles. I never saw them again.

I waited two weeks for the field to come to life. When the pickle plants started to grow, so did the weeds. I hoed and roto-tilled for days on end. When the pickles sprouted on the vines, I bought big burlap sacks at the feed mill to contain the bounty. Then I started picking.

Pickles can be mean and spiny critters. Especially the little ones, the ones that hide under leaves. But if you want to earn $2,000 an acre, it's those little pickles — the gherkin-size, no bigger than a baby's thumb —

that make your fortune. Takes a lot of those suckers to fill one brown sack.

Every other day, I had to deliver my fresh-picked pickles to a sorting station near Teeswater, a half-hour drive away. I would start picking at six a.m. before loading my bounty into the old pick-up truck at 4:30 and heading for the pickle depot. Rain or shine, it did not matter. Those gherkins could suck up rain drops and turn into full-blown cucumbers overnight.

I dreamed about pickles. Picking one whole row of perfect little gherkins was a fantasy. A whole row of eight-inch, slicing pickles was a nightmare.

My family thought I was nuts. Grandmother had once planted pickles, and all the aunts and uncles remembered the back-breaking work. Farm neighbours simply scrunched their foreheads and smiled. But with acres of nitrogen-powered pickles on the ground, there was nothing to do but pick.

The pickle depot opened at five p.m. I was never the first in line. Pickle people came in all shapes and sizes, just like their pickles. There were matrons in Buicks with pickles in their trunks. There were rusted out Volkswagens, barely more than roller-skates on wheels, with sacks full of pickles sagging out of the windows. Vans full of pickles, and pick-up trucks full of pickles and kids and barking dogs. Four strapping teenage boys who were working their way through university on pickle money would pull up with a manure spreader chock full of pickles. The line of pickle-laden vehicles spread down the county road like a misplaced caravan from *The Grapes of Wrath*. While we waited our turn to unload, we shared pickle stories and worried about leafy mould.

None of us had figured a way to harvest the pickles mechanically. Stories circulated about motorized carts built low to the ground. A picker could lie belly-down, turn on the ignition and scoot through the rows picking from either side. No one ever saw the contraption, but we could all imagine it.

In a cavernous shed, the pickle sorting machine clamoured and clacked for hours every night. It was a kind of triumph when you finally got to pour your pickle bags out onto the worn brown canvas that rolled and tossed the pickles to the pickle-grading slots. Two sisters kept a watchful eye for "bad uns," their short-nailed fingers grabbing wounded and distorted pickles as they bounced along the canvas. The littlest gherkins tumbled into big wicker baskets first, and the final Grade D cucumbers thudded at the end. Then thick-thighed farm boys hoisted the sorted pickles on a scale, shouting out weights and grades to the pickle accountant. Fixed, she sat at a maroon card-table and tapped the information into an ancient adding machine in a never-ending pat-pat-pat, dwarfed by the rattling of the machinery and the rolling thunder of thousands of pickles.

When all of my pickles were counted, I would take the yellow weigh slip and tuck it into the glove compartment just like all of the other pickle people. No one ever showed their yellow slip. It was the big secret, but we all knew that not one of us was going to pocket $2,000 an acre.

I picked tons of pickles that summer. I picked pickles until my hands were green. I even smelled faintly like a pickle. When the pickle station closed in September, I still had hundreds of pickles in the field. Nobody wanted to buy my pickles. None of the neighbours wanted my pickles; they already had a few in the garden. My parents politely took two quart baskets. I gave away a few more thanks to a sign at the end of the lane. Before me sat a pickle patch that could have garnished every restaurant plate in Toronto for two weeks, and they had no place to go.

So, I started canning. I ended up with five dozen quart jars of Aunt Marion's dill pickles before I finally quit. The cold cellar shelves groaned with the weight of pickles. I had dilled more pickles than a person could eat in three lifetimes. After that, anyone visiting the farm was not allowed to leave without taking at least one jar of dill pickles as a "memento." Customers who bought my freezer lamb and capons thought it was very sweet of me to include a jar of home-made pickles with their order. I gave dill pickles as Christmas gifts. I gave dill pickles as shower gifts. And I ate a lot of dill pickles.

The kicker arrived a few months after the frost had laid the leftover pickles and their vines to rest. A cheque in the mail came from my pickle boss. I savoured the feel of the envelope as I walked up the lane that autumn day, trudging past the pickle field where I had passed so many back-breaking days.

Even a cheque that realized the dream of $2,000 an acre would not have seemed enough. I knew exactly what the pickles had cost me, from the seed to the kids' bikes, to the burlap sacks, and the new tire for the old truck and the gas to keep it rolling. It was the most rude exercise in subtraction that I have ever done. All told, the whole effort earned me a total of $23.16. I did not tell anyone this sad state of affairs, because I knew that somewhere out there a joker was waiting to tell me that I was lucky that I did not lose money.

It has been nearly 15 years since my "pickle summer," and I still cannot look at a jar of dill pickles without cringing. When I come to the cucumber page in a seed catalogue, I turn it quickly.

I guess everyone who moves to the country has to make their own mistakes. Mine was ambition founded in greed, which blinded me to those silly little words "up to" in small print before the bold-faced pickle fantasy of $2,000 an acre.

There is nothing wrong with boldly going where few farmers have dared to go. It is the boldest of individual farmers in this country who have given us some of its greatest wealth. Think of John and Allan MacIntosh toiling to create that one special tree that grew the firmest, juiciest red apples they had ever encountered. Think of scientist Charles Saunders chewing his way through hundreds of kernels of wheat before discovering the grain that made Canada the breadbasket of the world.

But when you see a little advertisement in the local paper that promises $2,000 an acre for growing anything, think twice. It could land you in a real pickle.

ROY ROGERS AND ME

PEOPLE MOVE TO the country for all kinds of reasons from altruism to economics to sanity, but when you get right down to it I think what swayed me was the notion that I could have a horse.

I was practically weaned watching *National Velvet*. My favourite childhood storybook was *Black Beauty*. And while my other little school friends talked about honourable career goals such as nursing or teaching, I wanted to be a cowboy.

The other kids may have known the names of the top scorers in the NHL, but I knew that the Cisco Kid's horse was named Diablo.

My mother took me horseback riding for the first time when I was five. We were on a family trip through the Tennessee hills and there just happened to be a stable at the roadside and it just happened to have a trail ride.

Mother was always game for adventure, so while my father leaned warily against an old rail fence, I found myself being hoisted aboard a large, broad palomino horse which was outfitted with a pony saddle to suit my size. I looked like a pea on an elephant, but I felt like Roy Rogers.

It turned out to be quite a trail ride. We went up a mountain, threading our way on a slender path that was edged by a substantial drop-off. Mother kept wanting to stop to check on me, but there simply was no place to stop and I was having a great time hanging onto the reins and chatting away with the trail guide who was riding behind me. Mother did not seem to understand that going up and down the mountain was what these horses did for a living.

Coming down the mountain was the best part of the ride because the horses had gravity on their side and the promise of a moment of privacy at their feed bucket once they got back to the barn.

My horse, old Thunder, trotted along quite smartly while I flopped in the saddle like a bean bag hanging on for dear life. That was the first time I felt the special communion that exists between horse and rider.

I spent the next 10 years hooked on horses, and some of my happiest memories are of summers spent on horseback from dawn till dusk. I learned a lot about spirit and patience from those half-ton animals. Then I turned 15 and discovered that boys were also animals.

Somewhere between the discovery of boys, the pursuit of education and the aspirations of a career, horses side-stepped out of my life. But when I saw this farm in a weak moment with a real estate agent, the one thing that clinched the sale was a small barn that looked just about the right size for a box stall.

Of course, I didn't want to be too obvious. So I bought some sheep, took courses at the University of Guelph, planted crops and learned the art of stacking a hay mow before I made my move.

All the ad said was "Palomino mare for sale." I just thought I would take a look. She was perfect.

I have loved many horses from my uncle's massive gentle Percherons to the roughest buckskin bronco with a mean streak, but when the palomino mare set off in a canter that rolled like a gentle wave I knew that I had found a truly significant other.

Lady is the kind of horse you can ride with a halter and a rope and turn just by shifting your weight. She will allow anyone to ride her. I can put a five-year-old on her bare back and count on her not to do anything foolish. If a grown idiot decides to handle her roughly, she will give him the ride of his life until he smartens up or finds himself tossed into the manure pile.

Her instincts about people are as unerring as her ability to find a hidden carrot in a back pocket.

My faithful steed is now 16 years old. She still whinnies like a filly and prances like a showgirl. She has given me one daughter who is her spitting image, and together they roam the pastures making idiots out of each other. The young one is spoiled and she needs a lot of work, but old Lady is as dependable and smooth as the day I met her.

We do not hit the all-day trails as much now as we did in days gone by. Lady seems to prefer watching her daughter trot smartly in the exercise ring, but she is still game for fording a stream and corralling renegade sheep.

If she gives me another foal, she will have more than earned her hay.

Altruism and economics aside, there is a simple earthly comfort in greeting the day with a welcoming nuzzle from a golden horse. It does not guarantee sanity, but it does make some of the daily tribulations easier to accept.

All I have to do is fall prey to the lure of that gently swaying back and swing my leg up and grab a hunk of mane and — bingo! — I feel just like Roy Rogers again.

THE EARLY BIRD CATCHES
THE WORM-PICKER

ONE OF THE mythic stereotypes about life on a
farm is that the cock crows at dawn, triggering the
happy farmer into a joyful tumble out of bed to do
chores. I have had crazed roosters that crow at four
a.m., and at that time of morning I'm not ready to
tumble anywhere. The fact is, roosters crow anytime
they want. Light can trigger their crowing, but roosters
do not differentiate between moonlight, sunlight or, as
it happens, flash light.

My friend Ron had an on-going war with marauding worm-pickers. One of his back fields was flat and
fertile, perfect ground for night-crawlers. On a moist
summer night, he was driving home from a late meeting and saw an unfamiliar van parked on the concession
road beside his field. Half-a-dozen worm-pickers with
tin cans strapped to their waists and flashlights
mounted on their caps were feverishly harvesting a

bounty of limbless fish-bait. When Ron stopped to confront them they leapt over his fence and drove off.

Installing a "no trespassing" sign did no good. The pickers were nimble and quick. The fenceline was sagging, and Ron was starting to boil at the illicit harvest of "his" worms. The more he thought about the problem, the madder he got. No one from the police to his neighbours could control their mirth when Ron went on a "worm rustling" rant.

"What are you going to do? Catch 'em slime-handed," joked one of his erstwhile buddies.

In the coffee shop, the fellows who fish the local streams would trade stories about what lure or which fly was working. Then as Ron strolled by, they'd let it be known in loud voices that the only thing that was really catching fish was "Pride of Ron." When Ron found out that good worms were selling for more than a dime apiece, it pushed him over the edge.

Although he wasn't about to get into the business, he started thinking of worms as money in the ground. He installed a strand of barbed wire to protect his worms and his fences, but the night-crawler vigilantes clipped their way through it with wire-cutters. That was tantamount to a declaration of war.

When Ron asked his neighbour, Derek, if he could borrow the meanest bull in his barn as a worm protector, it was apparent that he had reached the end of his tether. He was thinking dangerous thoughts. He had even been overheard talking to veterans at the Legion about minefields.

"You want to catch them, not kill them," Derek offered, hoping that he was right. "What you want is an alarm system that no one would suspect."

Derek's wife, Kathy, raises prize-winning chickens and she clued them into the rooster defence. In half-an-hour they'd constructed a two-rooster-capacity cage made of chicken wire. They placed it in an unobtrusive stand of tall grass at the edge of the field and installed a pair of Kathy's cockerels.

Two days later, there was a light afternoon rain. It was just enough to call all crawlers to the surface at midnight. Ron notified the authorities to be on call, because he was certain he would be worm rustled that night. He wanted back-up.

Sure enough, in the dead of night those roosters started crowing their beaks off. Ron called the cops at the first crow. Derek was roused from his bed to block the worm-pickers' escape route at one end of the concession road, and Ron rushed to close off the other end.

By the time the boys-in-blue arrived, the worm-pickers were cowering beside their van. There were kids and women and little old men in the crew. Many of them did not speak English, and all of them were scared to death. Ron decided to let them off the hook. If there was a profit being made in worm picking, it was obvious that this motley crew of fish-bait rustlers was not getting the lion's share.

Under the glare of the headlights of assorted friends and passersby who gathered to witness the worm-picker bust, Ron did a reasonable pantomime explanation of his concern about fence damage. The confiscated worms were returned to the flat, fertile field. Remorse and apologies were expressed. With a stern warning, the rag-tag worm-pickers were sent on their way.

"They never saw it coming," chuckled Ron, as he regaled the coffee shop with the tale. "They might as well have rung my doorbell. As soon as those roosters caught sight of those flashlights they wear on their heads, they started crowing as though their were six suns in the sky."

Ron's worms have thrived without intrusion ever since. His fences are straight and stalwart. He still has the rooster cage and Kathy sold him a couple of big-time strutters for the barnyard, just in case. As the saying goes — the early bird catches the worm. But if you want to catch worm-pickers — get a rooster.

THE ORANGE DUMP TRUCK AND OTHER AUCTION NIGHTMARES

THERE IS NOTHING like an auction for drama, entertainment, warm pop and organized confusion. Particularly if you want to buy something that you never thought you would ever feel a need to own. If your Tupperware collection is missing that one final element to reach completion, if you just can't own enough used waffle irons or if you are constantly in fear of running out of anything from pillowcases to jackhammers — a country auction is about as close to nirvana as you may ever come.

When I first moved to the country, every auction in my area seemed like a potential gold mine. People smart enough to be retiring from the business I was getting into were having auctions that served as a great repository both in terms of value and information.

At an auction you can ask questions about farm machinery that you have never seen before. More often than not, there will be someone leaning against it who can not only tell you what the contraption does, but also provide some insight on whether or not the particular model you are looking at can be serviced within a 50-kilometre radius. Sometimes you can also garner a mechanical and repair history of the implement in question, along with theories about its ability to ever function in the future.

Of course, you must be wary because disinformation can also form part of the auction mentality. Somehow items that were "in good working order" the day before a sale have a nasty habit of falling apart the day after a sale.

Also, the definition of "good working order" sometimes stretches the envelope of reality. A friend of mine bought a stone picker at an auction and it does work. Unfortunately, it works at twice the speed anyone would expect. Stories about auction bargains are often like fish tales. The bargain seems to grow larger with each telling, but that is half the fun.

Over the years I have had some good fortune, but I have yet to bid on a cookie jar containing enough money to pay the mortgage. That is only one of many stories I have heard — and it always makes me look twice when an auctioneer holds up an innocent-looking cookie jar.

Then, of course, there was the day the 1952 orange Dodge dump truck ended up in my yard, courtesy of a bidder cursed with auction fever.

I took a male companion to a farm auction and made the mistake of letting him wander off alone.

While I waited patiently for the auctioneer to hold up an old pickle crock, my fellow fell into the company of some farmer neighbours who were camped out on the other side of the barn where the machinery was being auctioned. I guess they spotted the city slicker and decided to have some fun because the next thing he knew they were offering him a little sip of something from the swish barrel out behind the chicken shed.

I bid about as far as I was prepared to go on the crock, and added a few extra bids for good measure in the ritual process of "bidding up." This is a form of "if I can't have it you are going to pay dearly" kind of auction revenge. Then I wandered off to find my friend.

There was a lot of machinery for auction. Rows of hay bines, wagons, manure spreaders and such. Smack dab in the middle of the row was a huge old dump truck painted cadmium orange. I heard a shout go up as it was auctioned and then the crowd moved on.

As I scanned the human mass, I saw my urban buddy and managed a wave. He fairly bounded across the field, grinning from ear to ear and positively glowing from his venture behind the chicken coop.

Sure enough, he had become the joyful owner of an uncertified, engine-seized, ancient orange dump truck.

The story was rather jumbled, but it seemed his newfound friends had told him it actually worked, but no one else knew that it did. They had also told him that it would not sell for more than 60 dollars because everyone just thought it was scrap. So the boys dared him to buy it, and he did — for just 55 bucks.

The boys were rolling with laughter by this time and as they ambled out the laneway they were snickering heartily at my dilemma. After all, what do you do with a dump truck that hasn't worked for a quarter of a century?

It all worked out in the end. My neighbour Elmer, who collects old dump trucks for usable parts, traded me a new hitch on my pick-up for the orange nightmare. Then he turned around and sold the antique ram-head hood ornament for 125 dollars.

My foolish friend recovered from the swish with fond memories of owning a dump truck for a day, and I vowed never to allow city slickers to wander off at auctions.

THE RITE TO THE SILENCE
OF THE LAMBS

AS SPRING GIVES way to summer, I find myself wearing ear muffs. The time has come to wean the lambs from their mothers. Neither ewes nor lambs nor neighbours enjoy this process in animal husbandry.

When the lambs have reached a certain age and a certain size, they are simply too big to be butting up to their old mother and demanding milk. They have learned to eat grass, hay and grain. Instead of playing all day long, it is time for them to go about the serious business of growing up.

This is often easier said than done.

It is a stressful time for all concerned, so I try to approach it methodically and prepare for all eventualities. What I would really like to do is complete the task and book into a motel in Rangoon until the screaming is over.

Separating ewes from their lambs is one trick. I herd them through a chute and divert their courses into one area for lamb containment and one for ewes. But there is always one clever lamb who has learned to jump straight in the air and bound over fence tops. And there is usually one young ewe who has figured out a way to turn herself around in the smallest of spaces in an attempt to return to her overgrown off-spring.

I remove the ewes to a far paddock, but it is still close enough that they can hear the lambs' cries and bleat their own moans of separation. For the next few days, they will be fed last year's dry hay and given scant water. It may sound like a punishment, but it serves to help them stop producing milk in a process called "drying up."

In the barn the lambs cry like lost children. They nibble aimlessly at their fine alfalfa and ignore their molasses-scented grain. Some of them have louder baas than others, and there is always one little heartbreaker with a mournful soprano.

You cannot pat a lamb on the head and tell it everything is going to be all right. You cannot explain to a sad-faced ewe that her udder is not a punching bag, and she needs to get back into shape and get on with her life. You cannot reason with sheepish passion.

The screaming usually lasts for about 48 hours. Then the ewes go off to their pastures. The lambs settle into their barn and exercise paddock. And the shepherd gets a good night's sleep.

It is a sort of rite of passage. After they are weaned, the lambs seem to have lost their innocence. The young rams play tougher, and the young ewes become more docile. They are no longer "cute." They are eating machines. Over the next few weeks everything from their feed conversion and heredity will come under scrutiny to determine the "keepers" from the market lambs. This is a business, after all, and as much as I love my lambs, they are not pets. My farming neighbours understand that the few evenings of bawling is part of my operation, but less experienced folks could well imagine that I had opened a 24-hour sheep torture chamber.

At a shepherds' meeting a few years ago, the topic was "Animal Rights and Preparing for Activists." Perhaps we were ahead of our time, but one never knows when some vegetarian pop singer or ballerina or poet is going to announce to the world that shepherds are cruel and lamb chops are the consequence.

Indeed, it turned out that one shepherd had already been a victim of misunderstanding. A neighbour, who was a recent urban transplant, had heard the weaning of the lambs and decided it sounded more like a scene from *The Silence of the Lambs*.

Instead of inquiring politely about the well-being of the livestock, the neighbour called the Humane Society. You can imagine the outrage of the gentle shepherd when an inspector visited with the suspicious neighbour in tow.

I told this tale of woe to a friend who raises cattle and she laughed. Her farm is also a bed and breakfast, and most of her close neighbours are recent arrivals to the country who do not farm. She knew the cows and calves would raise a ruckus, so she had closed her farm for visitors while the weaning took its course. After the first gruesome night of choral mooing, she decided she should explain the situation to the neighbours and assure them that an end was in sight.

Her first stop was at the home of a young couple with a baby. The woman was weary-eyed, and my friend feared the worst.

No, she had not been bothered by cow sounds at night. She had been weaning her baby and he cried all night.

THE HUMPS OF THE HOLSTEIN

I LIKE TO go to the feed mill in Holstein, about eight kilometres from my farm.

It is an old-style feed mill, with huge timber rafters, the smell of grain in the dusty air and a regular sort of tricolour cat lounging around waiting for the sign of a single mouse.

At the mill they will mix up any sort of feed you might want and give some advice to anyone willing to listen. Big blue salt blocks are lined up against one wall, and notes are posted on a huge beam listing the various mixtures for dairy cows, pigs and poultry.

There are other feed mills closer to me than Holstein, but none that has the same charm.

I guess a lot of it has to do with the village of Holstein itself. It is a really nice place to visit even on a rainy day. There aren't any subdivisions in Holstein, just houses that have big front lawns and more rocking chairs per porch than I've ever seen.

Main Street is just a stretch of road with a gas station and a couple of garages with signs that proclaim the owner's name. The general store is appropriately called "The General Store" and you can buy everything from pork chops to paper clips there. Holstein even has its own clothing line of sweatshirts and T-shirts, featuring its namesake black and white cow.

A stream bisects the town, and there is a big park which is home to many a family reunion and baseball tournament. People still tell fish tales about the monster pike that once got trapped near the dam.

And Holstein has a camel, a regulation two-hump model named Baxter, who is featured is every local parade. He is owned by a local farmer who established a sort of wildlife preserve along with his sheep and cattle and poultry farm. At one time he had a herd of bison, but that ended when one of the beasts decided to attack him on his tractor.

There are quite tame white-tailed deer in a wooded setting at the edge of the road, and many a local child has marveled at their velvety noses while feeding them a handful of grain. Zebras and elk have graced the fields, and peacocks seem to free-range in the ditches.

Tuesday and Friday are big days for traffic in Holstein because those are the only days that the local credit union is open. It is a two-woman operation with a lot of personality. The tellers know me by name and there is always time for a chat about the weather.

On Sunday the church bells peal and the parishioners gather like something out of an old movie.

A kind of infectious whimsy is always in the air when you drive into this village, and a palpable sense of indeterminate history seems to overtake the sensibilities. I guess that is why I never buy too much feed at one time.

There is something secretly wonderful about knowing that when I make up my official morning chore list of "Things to Do Today," I can write "pick up grain" and "do banking" and know that it also means I get to give a camel a carrot.

Rub-a-Dub-Dub, Two Sheep and No Tub

You never know how dirty and smelly a sheep really is until you wash one. I discovered this one fine summer day when I was getting two ram lambs ready to go to a sheep show.

The rams looked clean. Sheared in the spring, they came out looking as white as lilies. Then they cavorted in the pasture in all kinds of weather. I thought of them as naturally rain-washed and sun-dried creatures. But going to a sheep show requires more primping than Mother Nature had in mind. In fact, it practically requires a beautician's licence.

When I told a few of my senior shepherd friends that I planned to show my fine rams, they all had tidbits of advice.

"Walk them on a halter every day, or they'll run you around the ring," said one sage. So I made a rope halter and started taking the boys for a daily turn around the paddock. I learned to wear old clothes while doing this, since the young rams seemed to get a kick out of dragging me around. They were outlaws. So I named them after my favourite country and western renegades, Willie Nelson and Waylon Jennings.

"Get them to stand good and square" was another piece of wisdom. How this guy thought I was going to get the darn rams to hold still when I couldn't even get them to heel, I do not know.

Then came the concept of "fitting" the sheep for the show ring, an exercise that comes close to preparing a model for a Paris runway. In the course of events, I learned that before a perfectly good sheep could enter a show ring its feet had to be manicured, its wool cleaned and fluffed and its head suitably shined. I swear that if sheep had eyebrows, someone would have told me to pluck them.

I was about ready to abandon the whole idea when I thought of Judy, my shearer. She has been showing sheep all her life, and in her spare time she teaches 4-H'ers the tricks of the trade. Hearing my dilemma, Judy agreed to "fit" the rams, but I would have to do the washing. I felt sort of like the shampoo person for Vidal Sassoon.

I bought a big jug of gooey, greasy livestock shampoo and lined up the garden hose. The day was hot and ripe for lathering. Willie knew the game was afoot when I flopped him to the ground in the corral and trimmed his tiny perfect hooves with garden pruners. Sheep do not like having this done. Waylon responded by trying to kick the bejeebbers out of me.

Wool soaks up a lot of water. By the time I got

them drenched to the skin, Willie and Waylon were literally wet blankets and they smelled like dirty sweaters. I lathered them up, down and sideways. Dirt and grime flowed out of their wool. Mother Nature was obviously not fastidious when it came to rain-washing sheep.

Before they started sun-drying, I called Judy to find out whether cream rinse was in order.

"What? You've just washed them once?" she asked. I winced as dribbles of shampoo and grunge caked on my face. "Wash 'em again and be sure you scrub their equipment. That's what the judges will be looking at for sure."

I might not have been raised on a farm, but by now I knew enough animal anatomy lingo to catch her drift. Off I went with hose in hand to re-wash my rams and consider the most mannerly method of scrubbing their "equipment."

The boys seemed to relish a second chance at the massage that goes with a full-fleece shampoo. Willie mellowed right out when I lathered his privates, but the cold-water rinse put some bounce back into his attitude.

By the time I was ready to tackle Waylon's scrotum, I felt that I was getting the hang of the whole sheep-washing thing. I was down on my knees scrubbing away like an old washerwoman when I heard a car barreling up the laneway.

It was the dreaded insurance agent.

There was nowhere to run, nowhere to hide. He was at the fence in a flash and I was fully exposed.

"Picked a nice day to wash the flock," said the

cheeky little monkey. I focused all my energy on the job at hand.

"Just need you to initial something on the truck insurance policy," he snickered, waving his ball-point as though a soaking wet woman shampooing the nether parts of a male sheep had three hands.

Waylon let out a guttural baa. I clenched my teeth in anticipation of some blinding display of sopho-moronic wit.

"Guy's got a good set of windpipes, heh, heh."

Fully lathered, I rose from the muck and reached for his dangling pen. Waylon gave me a playful butt from behind.

"Looks like you might need something a bit more in the collision insurance department. Heh, heh," he chortled.

"Wrong," I offered impassively, as I swirled my initials on the designated page.

I expected him to leave, laughing all the way. Wrong again. As I commenced the rinse cycle on Waylon, the insurance agent clung to the fence as though he had front row seats at a Tijuana side-show.

"Might need some extra coverage, though," I shouted back at him. Without even looking, I knew those were sweet words to his perky, insurance-agent ears.

"Whaddya have in mind? Sheep blanket coverage, heh, heh," he crowed.

"How about All-Perils," I said turning quickly, hose in hand and nozzle adjusted to full-stream ahead. Got him dead on around the mid-section before he could run.

Judy was pleased with my ram laundry job. She didn't say much, but I got the feeling that she would have graded me well in her 4-H class. As casually as though they were born with halters on, the boys walked obediently to her trimming stand and posed stock still, legs squarely planted, backs straight and chins up. Using her clippers, hand trimmers and various combs, Judy methodically tailored their wool to the specifications of the show ring. A little off here and a bit plumped up there made a world of difference. She used a pump-spray bottle of water and other secret ingredients to work the wool into place. I caught a glimpse of a jar of Dippity Doo.

When the rams were finally "blocked," we stood back to admire her handiwork.

"Bit rough but we're getting there," said Judy. To me they already had the stamp of Grand Champion on their shiny black heads.

MANURE SPREADING DAY

BETWEEN HAYING AND harvesting, summer can move fairly quickly on a farm. The garden always needs weeding, grass grows like weeds and it becomes nearly impossible to keep up with the zucchinis. Cucumbers may grow from gherkin-size to salad slicers overnight, but if you don't catch a zucchini in time it can grow into a small canoe.

Today I was in the midst of contemplating taming the zucchinis when Jim's Manure arrived. Complete with two manure spreaders and a front-end loader.

I never know exactly when to expect Jim's Manure. The machines are busy from April through November, travelling all over, cleaning out barns and spreading you-know-what over the fields. Jim just puts your name down on his list and when he gets to you — well, he gets to you. Jim himself drove one of the spreaders this year.

First he surveyed the job, in the process lamenting not having taken the day off to go fishing. It seems I'm a small fish in a big pond in terms of manure spreading jobs. But just consider the fact that one of my sheep management books suggests that half a ton of sheep produce eight and a half tons of manure annually. Roughly translated that means that my flock of 50 or so ewes had produced more that 42 tons of excrement since Jim's last visit, and approximately 35 percent of that was solid waste with nowhere to go until Jim arrived.

Jim and crew got right to work. I don't know who invented the manure spreader, but the light bulb that flashed above that person's head must have been quite something.

A spreader is a sort of a big iron box on wheels with paddles that toss the manure out the back. I don't know how the thing works, but pretty soon all three spreaders were spitting last year's sheep left-overs all over the pasture. It is a very organic business.

It took about five hours to finish the job, and Jim figured he'd have just enough time left in the day to make it to his secret fishing hole, where a big bass had been playing hard to get for weeks.

I was not so lucky. Although machines can do wonders, they can't get into the corners of a barn. So I spent the rest of the day up to my boot-tops in sheep poop — shoveling as fast as I could. It is kind of mindless work. I try not to think about what I'm doing while I'm doing it.

Good things can happen in the detritus of a job like that. For instance, I found a long-lost screwdriver, a great chunk of rubber hose and my trusty Buck knife

— all of which had somehow wound up buried in the sheep pen.

Now the barn is clean and I am about as filthy as my Buck knife. The sheep are confused by a landscape without a manure pile, and the pasture field has been fertilized within an inch of its life.

My muscles tell me that they have done an honest day's work. There will still be weeds in the garden tomorrow, and grass to cut, and zucchini to be plucked and relished. But maybe I'll take a cue from Jim of Jim's Manure, find myself a cool bank on the river, forget about sheep and just go fishing. There are options on the farm.

FEAR AND LOATHING FROM THE GARDEN OF EDEN

THE SNAKES SEEM to be in full form this year.

Since early spring I have been catching them napping in the full sun and finding shed skins around the base of trees where they like to rub.

They surprise me now and then when I am walking through long grass, but I cannot get too excited about a garter snake. Call it Freudian, but I have been a snake fan since I was a little kid and lived near a ravine which all manner of snake, salamander and newt called home.

My parents, who seemed to have nothing for or against snakes, were wise enough to foster my early childhood interest in species other than my own. We would go on family outings to creek beds, and while the others were having a picnic, I would be turning over rocks in search of squirmy things to bring home for further examination.

Mother put her foot down when she found the bathtub filled with tadpoles, but as long as I cleaned my terrarium she was amenable to gathering a few earth-worms from the garden to help feed my "collection." Dad introduced me to an elderly man who was a naturalist, and we would spend hours talking about everything from what happened to the dinosaurs to the changing colours of chameleons. Those were the days before *Sesame Street* and Nintendo.

By the time I entered grade three, I had accumulated about 35 domestic snakes through zoos and "snake trades" and scavenging. I seemed to have a knack for acquiring snakes named Samson who had to be renamed Delilah the moment they gave birth.

My snakes-in-the-basement thing tended to divide my little friends into two distinct groups — those who wanted to come for visits at my house after school and those who would not even attend a birthday party in a house that harboured snakes. This was my first encounter with irrational fear and intolerance. It could have been a lot worse. The snakes were not offended.

When I grew out of the herpetological hobby, my pets were released into suitable habitats, where I hope they lived happily ever after.

Moving to the farm provided an opportunity to reacquaint myself with creatures of all kinds, including my legless buddies. A farm can be a hazardous place for snakes. I discovered this after routinely ploughing a field and churning up a few garters in the process. And then, of course, there is the fear and loathing syndrome.

Early on, while rebuilding an old cedar rail fence in a back pasture with some helpers, I chanced across a very large brown snake with an interesting black geometric pattern. Even coiled, I could tell it was about three feet long. When it seemed to rattle its tail, the others jumped back and hid behind the pick-up. Then one macho man got a rail about 10 feet long and tried poking the snake. Its head snapped back as though striking.

A general consensus formed among the fearful that they were confronting a deadly rattlesnake, but I just didn't buy it. I didn't see any rattles on the big snake's tail, or any fangs. Furthermore, no one had ever heard of rattlesnakes in the neighbourhood.

I made a rough sketch and ran back to my library to identify the snake. There are similarities of colouration between the massasauga rattler and the common milk snake — even overlaps in territory — but the milk snake is as harmless to humans as a garter snake. It is a well-adapted snake, however, and it copies the behaviour of a rattlesnake right down to vibrating its tail to make an intimidating warning sound when it is startled. Leave it alone and it goes about its business, the upside of which is keeping the rat population in balance. Altogether, the milk snake is about as dangerous as a pointed finger pretending it is an Uzi.

By the time I returned, the anti-snakers had killed it. No doubt the poor creature was as frightened of them as they were of it. It had tried to nonchalantly slither away and they perceived that as some form of sneak attack. When I chastised them for killing a simple milk snake, I was countered with a cockamamie story about "milk" snakes preying on the udders of dairy cows at night. Having tried my hand at milking, I can tell you that not even the most lackadaisical old cow would stand for such nonsense.

After that I heard a number of snake stories, most of them second- or third-hand and virtually all of them clouded in the kind of superstition that has hounded snakes ever since that alleged incident in the Garden of Eden.

For instance, I heard the one about snakes that bite hold of their tails and move across fields like self-propelled hula-hoops. The unspeakable viciousness of snakes was attested to by the belief that mother garter snakes will eat their babies at the approach of danger. However, my experience indicates that snakes are just like the rest of us, and when danger approaches they adopt the sensible position of "run away, run away." The fact is that if a full-term pregnant garter is killed and cut open, the unborn young may survive. Such is the stuff that creates old wives' tales.

You can generally challenge misinformation with correct information, but when it comes to snakes I have found that being "right" does not necessarily change attitudes. It's a lot like talking politics or religion.

Even though I can hold a snake and offer disbelievers the opportunity to touch it to prove that it is not slimy, they will still feel what they want to feel.

So now I keep my snakes to myself. My wild pregnant garters like to snooze on a rock pile overlooking the pond. Their young will be born — alive and slithering. They will abandon their mothers immediately and begin fending for themselves. Like everything else in nature they will become a part of a food chain — some will live but most will die. I think about snakes when the ploughs hit the fields, and I will never turn a harmless snake out of my garden.

Of Bulls and Variables

ONE MID-SUMMER DAY, I had a call from Big
Tom, a downtown friend who puts together deals. This
is the kind of a guy who makes money by generating
ideas on paper and letting other people buy into the
idea of trying them out. It is what you might call
"creative" work. Some of my farmer friends who are
out there bouncing through the fields on their tractors
baling hay might have another word for it.

Tom was generating an idea about farming. To do
this, he needed to create a model, showing profit and
loss and capital gain and depreciation, and all of those
other things that I'd rather not think about when the
strawberries need picking.

His model had cows and sheep and pigs and chickens, and he needed some advice about the sheep part.

"So how many pounds of lamb meat can I get from
one, whaddya-call-them — youses — in a year and how
much can I get per pound?" he asked.

Now I was once a city girl myself, and I always figured that if anyone would have an answer to a question that would be the soul of brevity — it would be a farmer, one close to the simplicity of nature. But 15 years on the farm has taught me that there is nothing simple about nature, and there is virtually no easy answer to any question about farming.

"Well, that depends," I answered, in the best tradition of my neighbour Hooter the horse farmer, who answers every question with a "depends" caveat. "It depends on what type of ewe you are breeding, what size of lamb you are marketing, when you are selling and who you are selling it to. For starters."

"Okay, okay, so there are variables," my eager friend replied. "Just give me a top end scenario."

We shuffled a few numbers around. We talked about the Dorset breed versus the Suffolk, the difference between Easter prices and August prices, and the dressed weight of a lamb as opposed to its live weight.

I could hear Big Tom pounding the numbers into his computer as we talked. Variables, these guys love variables. When I told Tom that one ram could probably service as many as 40 ewes, all he could say was "Wow."

"So, what have you got for pigs?" I asked, when we'd finished figuring out that there was hardly a penny of profit in sheep.

"Looks good so far," he said. "I start with one female pig called a sow, and she has two babies…"

I had to stop him before he got into the second year projections.

"Thomas," I interjected, "a breeding sow in my uncle's barn is usually good for at least 16 piglets a year."

"More variables, " he muttered.

The problem here is one I've seen before. There are a lot of variables to farming, and unless you investigate them one at a time, there's always a variable out there that leaves you looking like a model of lunacy. I've been there, seen it, done it too many times to be embarrassed anymore. Chalk it up to the 4-H Club slogan "learn by doing," but I always hope someone can tell me before I do it badly.

For instance, a lawyer I know once bought a farm as a country retreat. He had only good intentions for the buildings and the land. Contrary to what many people might think, he wasn't buying a tax dodge. So-called "dodges" are as mythical as the brown cow that gives chocolate milk. Truth be known, he was trying to buy some sanity with after-tax dollars.

The lawyer liked cows. He didn't want to start a cattle empire. He just liked the notion of having a few cows.

So he went to a neighbouring farm and bought a dozen of the colour that appealed to him. He put up fences, and he hired a lad to care for the cows. It gave him great pleasure to see the cows grazing in his fields.

Then came the question of breeding the cows. And all of a sudden, the lawyer became a farmer. "of course, I'm having them bred," he told the neighbours. And he asked for the name of the best bull seller around.

Like a lot of city folk who come to the country, this

was one urbanite who wasn't going to let country folk tell him what to do every inch of the way. They were his cows, goll-darn-it, and he was going to see that they were bred to the best darn bulls around.

Even though he was a lawyer, this guy had never seen a real bull in the flesh. Still, he spent a fine Saturday afternoon selecting bulls from a purebred breeder with a wall full of ribbons to show the excellence of his stock. He bought 12 bulls for his 12 cows and ordered them delivered the following weekend. Although the bull breeder attempted to explain the non-monogamous nature of cattle, the lawyer's insistence and the looming financial bonanza mitigated further protest.

When the truck pulled up, the lad who was tending the cows was a bit disconcerted.

"You can't put them out there, no way," he advised as the truck eased into the pasture field where the cows were grazing.

"My cows, my bulls, nature's way," said the lawyer, fully believing that the boisterous boys and the comely heifers would pair off equally and go quietly into the sunset to make little cows.

Well, all hell broke loose when the gates were opened. The bulls bolted like something out of a Merrill Lynch commercial — all wild and bucking, with fury in their crazed loins. The cows froze. Then the bulls decided to run at each other. After all, when a bull sees a dozen cows he wants to make each one his own, and he's not about to share with his brothers.

It took six good men and three good cutting horses

to straighten out the donnybrook that ensued. Some of the bulls were taken to isolation stalls in other barns and the rest were tethered by nose rings in the lawyer's barn. The cows just shook their heads in disbelief. The neighbours wandered off with a story they knew they could supper on for the next decade. The lawyer acknowledged that maybe he had taken on more bull than he could handle.

The lad selected one of the bulls as the herd sire, and the rest were sold at auction. But the lawyer never saw the fine calves that resulted. After the Great Bull Fiasco, he couldn't even go into a supermarket without hearing whispers behind him as the story spread.

He sold the farm and bought a ski chalet.

At least with skiing, you know that you only need one ski per leg.

I hope that Big Tom's farm model works out. The country can always use an infusion of capital from city people who want to get closer to nature and understand a few variables. But if Thomas ever calls me with a truckload of rams for sale, I'll be the first to tell him he's got the wrong number.

THE FARMER GETS A TAN

BY JULY THE first round of haying is complete and there is a sort of breathing period on the farm. In this window of time, I can actually block off time to ride the horse for fun, wander through the garden just to look at the way things are growing, and generally stop to smell the peonies.

Around this time of year, the level of water in the pond naturally drops. The frogs take over, plopping for cover when they hear footsteps. So this year I decided I would do something a little different — I would go to an actual beach.

At the beach you can always tell a farmer from the rest of the crowd. We are the ones with the unusual suntans. You will notice, for example, that a farmer will generally have an excellent tan on the back of the neck — just below the baseball cap line and just above the T-shirt line. Some pejorative folks would call it a "redneck," but a friend of mine calls it "farmer's neck syndrome." The tan stops where the T-shirt begins and proceeds again from some point just above the elbow.

The tan of the hand is another matter. When you handle bales of hay or straw, it is a good idea to wear a pair of durable gloves with the fingers removed so that the twine doesn't cut into your palm. Under a beating sun this leads to tanned digits and white hands. Likewise, since I don't tend to wear socks, my tan ends where the running shoes begin.

So when it came time to don my beachwear and sandals, I realized that I might just as well have tattooed "farmer" on my forehead.

Beach scenes are pretty much the same everywhere. Seagulls cruising overhead. The smell of hotdogs and burgers. Miles of faces in sunglasses and floppy hats. The lapping of water and the crunch of sand in your shoes — not a cow, chicken or sheep in sight or sound.

There were a lot of very good tans on the beach. In fact, there were some tans that looked darned professional. In contrast, my thighs and upper body were pale, my toes white and my knees and lower arms bronze. I realized that I stood out like a thistle in a wheat field.

To disguise myself just a bit, I decided to at least keep my baseball cap on while I set off for the shoreline. No one even noticed me. Small children did not ask their mothers why that lady had two skin colours. There was no giggling behind my back. No one asked me if I shouldn't be at home milking the cows.

Floating in the big water of Georgian Bay is different from drifting on a farm pond. There are waves that roll, and that faint feeling of undertow that comes with a horizon where water meets sky. I was casually practising my crawl stroke when an ambient wave caught hold of my baseball cap and washed it out of sight.

Half an hour later, I felt cooled enough to return to the beach. The water had rinsed away a lot of daily strife. Not once had I considered the plague of potato beetles in the garden, or contemplated the logistics of moving turkeys into a new pen, or dwelled on the cost-effectiveness of buying a post-hole digger versus renting one.

I had barely reached my towel when a young man with a perfect tan came bounding over.

"Think I found your hat, ma'am," he said. Producing a damp mess with a red brim. At least the colour was right.

I took the hat and examined it. Mine had come from a farm-equipment dealer and featured a tractor on it. But the sodden cap I held in my hands just had the words "Farmers Do it in the Hay." I'd been found out.

By then the bronzed boy had disappeared into the herd of tans. Some farmer left the beach hatless that day, but it wasn't me.

God Gave Us a Horse

IT WAS ONE of those glorious summer mornings. The sun was shining, a light breeze rippled through the maple trees and you could almost hear the corn growing in the field. So I slept in.

However, my companion "the Moose" had decided it was such a fine day that he would venture to take his annual horseback ride.

Moose is not what you would call diminutive and he is also not exactly an equestrian. These are two features that Lady the Horse spotted right off the bat. She is one of the smoothest riding horses I have ever sat on, but with Moose on board she turns into a stilt-legged trotting maniac. Thus the annual ride is generally brief and to the point.

So I was quite surprised when I rose from my bed to hear the thunder of galloping hooves beating a path to the front door. Breathless would appropriately describe the condition of both horse and rider. While Lady snorted her discontent, the Moose managed to wheeze: "Come quick! God has given us a horse."

Sure enough, tethered to a wild apple tree on the back 40 lane he had discovered a shiny brown horse.

While it has always been my fantasy that more horses would casually wander into my life, the only thing that people seem to freely deposit at a farmer's doorstep are unwanted dogs and cats.

We looked for signs of human tracks near the unknown horse and found a path worn into the cornfield. There we found, half-hidden, a polished black Mennonite buggy with the bridle and driving lines hanging from a tree branch.

The birds twittered from the trees; otherwise there were no signs of life around the buggy. Since we're both from the city, immediately our thoughts flew to foul play. There is a large Mennonite population in my area and so little is known about their religious ways and personal habits that prejudice occasionally surfaces and takes odd forms.

Mumbling about pranksters and red-necks, we prepared to take the horse back to our barn while we sought out its gentle, peace-loving owner who was probably attending a prayer meeting or helping with a community barn-raising.

Just as we were leaving, a rustle came from the bushes and a tousled, teenage Mennonite lad appeared. He was barefoot and buttoning his shirt. Sheepishly, he explained that he was new to the area and had not been aware that anyone lived here, so he had parked in the shade to cool off his horse for a few minutes.

Knowing something about horses and the deposits

that they make over a period of time, it occurred to me that the bone-dry horse had been cooling his heels for several hours.

Then we heard another rustle in the bushes, and out she came: an apple-cheeked lass of about 16, who busied herself with brushing grass from her long dark skirt while she thanked us for our concern about the horse.

Moose and I managed to walk halfway back to the barn before we dissolved into laughter. The next time God decides to give us a horse, I think we will call it Romance.

THE SOAKING BABY-DOLL DEFENCE

THE SHEEP HIT the front lawn at six a.m.

I awoke from the leaden sleep of someone who slogged 400 bales of hay into a dusty barn the day before to find all 50 woolly beggars eagerly foraging through the petunias.

By the time I hit the front door, a handful of lambs had taken over the porch of the farmhouse and secured rights to the leftover Kibble in the dog's dish. Stella the dog, a 100-pound hair-ball Akita who lives to eat, nearly had a heart attack but managed to refrain from chomping wool.

The sheep scattered like pool balls when they saw me. Something about being on the other side of the fence must charge them with adrenaline because even the old reliable ewes began bouncing around and kicking up their heels. The lambs divided into two squadrons: one dedicated to devouring geraniums and the other focused on discovering the garden.

The garden! All my neatly tended rows of green beans, peas, lettuce and sweet corn rising. There is a Chinese proverb that says to be happy for a week you take a new concubine. To be happy for a month you kill a pig. And to be happy for the rest of your life you build a garden. I have not tried the first two proverbial suggestions, but I heartily subscribe to the last.

In an instant I saw the ewes lift their heads from the petunias in unison. If they had been cartoon characters they would all have sported a light bulb turning on in the balloon above their small brains.

"Please," I begged them. "Not the garden!"

Sheep are not revolutionaries. They are not like chickens who will spend weeks plotting their way out of a coop, or pigs who will bide their time waiting for the instant a gate opens to make a squealing exit. Sheep do not make plans. But when they find themselves outside the fence, sheep are born anarchists.

The overthrow of my garden appeared inevitable.

Running about and screaming has never served me well with sheep. It seems to amuse them and provides them with an incentive to carry on exactly as they please.

I leapt barefoot into my trusty Wellingtons and pursued the only option that seemed quick at hand — the sprinkler system. I had laid perforated hoses throughout the vegetable rows in the early spring when I thought we might have a dry summer. Within seconds of turning on the tap, the garden sprouted with fine streams of H_2O.

Sheep hate surprises and it was only a minute before they bounded back to the gravel lane in confusion.

Five minutes and a pail of grain later, the whole crew was quietly returned to the field. Sheep will follow you anywhere for a handful of oats. And they do follow like sheep. As soon as one ewe heard the rustle of grain in the pail, the rest trailed along behind with petunias still clinging to their lips as they fertilized the lawn at will.

With no time to spare I settled into repairing a two-foot gap in a cedar rail fence that had allowed just enough space for the entire flock to belly-walk their way to freedom. Sheep are creatures of habit who do not take defeat well, and petunias hold an odd allure for them.

The sun was at about seven o'clock when I finished. Dusting off my knees, I walked back to my soaking garden and cooled off in the misty spray from the sprinkler system. The sheep had been outwitted again, and I felt like the Schwartzkopf of garden defence strategy.

Stella sat grimly on the front porch beside her empty dish casting me baleful and inquisitive looks. I guess she has never seen a soaking wet woman wearing pink baby-doll pyjamas and Wellington boots eat a freshly washed carrot so early in the morning.

OWLS IN THE CHICKEN COOP

THERE IS A pair of Great Horned Howls that live in the bush at the back of the farm. I hear them "who-whoing" at night. It is a low, haunting sound that reminds me of sitting around the Girl Guide fire and telling ghost stories.

I have only seen the owls a few times on moonlit nights, swooping across the pasture fields looking for their prey. They are big birds and they hunt in silence. When they spot something tasty moving in the grass they descend on it with surprising speed, talons first. It is quite a dramatic sight, powerful and terrifying, but somehow defined by an overwhelming grace.

I like having the owls around, but I wish they would stick to the pastures for their evening meals and stay away from my chickens.

I must admit that I am not a big fan of the white Leghorn chickens that I raise for meat. They are noisy and stinky and I have no doubt that their IQ is a heck of a lot lower than their body temperature.

But, whatever endearing qualities these creatures may lack in life, there is really nothing quite like a plump, farm-grown, corn-finished roaster chicken to make Sunday dinner something special. So it should come as no surprise that I am willing to put up with their cannibalism, stupid chicken tricks and constant squawky crowing. I see them as much more than a life-support system for the elusive owl population.

The problem is that I started out with 100 chicks but I am now down to 89 full-feathered juvenile birds thanks to Mr. and Mrs. Horned Owl.

Chicken brains must be some sort of owl caviar, because they only take the head. As you can imagine, it is most disconcerting to discover the decapitated victims of these flying guillotines.

Local farmers have advised me that the only solution is to lock the chickens up at night. This would be well and good but my chickens are the organic type, and they free-range in their fenced area. They do not come when they are called and they are not partial to curfews.

A large maple bough shades the open-sided coop where they roost at night, and I suspect it provides the owls with an ideal look-out and launching post, but I am not prepared to cut it down.

I have talked with my local conservation officer, who advised me that since the birds are preying on my livestock I could legally shoot them. Unfortunately, everything I learned in my hunter education course would indicate that firing a shotgun at night is not a safe practice.

And I do like the owls. Somehow I cannot rationalize reducing them to puffs of feathers because they like chicken as much as I do.

The nature narc told me that it is fairly difficult to trick an owl into a humane trap, and they are not shy about dining out in well-lit areas. However, they do not care for noise and they are wary about attacking in the same spot when things physically change.

That's when I thought of the sleigh bells and the pink flamingos.

Covering the chicken range would be a costly affair, but if there is one thing I have accumulated yards of, it is baler twine. And the one thing I could not resist at a garage sale was a basketful of jumbo-sized sleigh bells.

I rigged strands of twine across the chicken range and tied bells to each strand. Then I took out the pair of plastic pink flamingos that have been living in my basement since my farm helpers parked them on top of the manure pile as a joke. I planted the flamingos in the chicken range at dusk and left the chickens to enjoy sweet dreams while the sleigh bells jingled in the breeze.

Nothing happened for a week. I kept moving the flamingos and ignoring what I am certain was the sound of chickens laughing. Finally, one night around midnight there arose such a clatter that I went to my window to see what was the matter.

Suffice it to say, the bells were ringing for me and my owls.

I still hear the owls at night, but they seem to have altered their diet and returned to foraging in the pastures and fresh-mown hayfields. And thanks to sleigh bells and pink flamingos, my chickens can keep their tiny heads — for the time being at least.

Fall

GETTING THE LINGO AND THE LAY OF THE LAND

IT WAS MY first autumn in the country and I was preparing for winter. Everyone said we were headed for a doozie. One farmer could tell by the texture of his cattle's coats and another cited the early departure of the geese. An organic farmer spent hours explaining the physical changes in the appearance and depth of earthworms. Obviously, I was not the only one with winterization in mind. The plumber was so busy that he could only make time to set up a heated water bowl in the barn after dinner. The sun went down and I waited, watching for headlights to wind up the lane. No one came.

When I called the next day, he told me he had been at the farm after dinner, but no one was there. He looked in the barn and figured he knew where to put the water bowl. There was no question he had visited. He described the dogs, the sheep and the scarecrow in the garden. I felt as though I was living in the Twilight Zone. How could I have missed him?

"Well, I was there about 1:30," he said. I thought for a moment.

"Sorry," I offered, "I was out because I thought you were coming after dinner."

"I did," he said.

That was my first lesson in rural-speak. In my part of the country, dinner means lunch and supper means dinner. Lunch is a big midday spread that you have on a weekend with family or friends attending. Lunch is also the sandwiches, salads and desserts that "ladies" bring to evening parties. It is usually served around 11:00 at night when things begin to wind down.

Country language can become a complicated affair. Nothing is quite as simple as just a "chicken." For example, there are pullets, which are female chickens that are old enough to lay eggs. Then there are layers, which are chickens that are in the process of laying eggs. There are roasters (which are usually roosters) that you grow into Sunday-supper-sized birds, and there are broilers that commercial growers feed to supply fast-food restaurants and such. Then there are capons, which are roosters minus hormones, which means they grow big breasts like hens. The whole lot of them are called fowl.

The local newspaper carries all of the social news. If I want to know who took tea with whom or who is planning a reunion or having a baby shower in my area, I must look under the column labeled "Little Ireland."

It seems the Irish first pioneered the neighbourhood. Although it is now populated by everyone from Mennonites to Portuguese and Scots, the social identity is still related to the century-old cemetery down the road. Similarly, ancient school districts that have long since gone the way of amalgamation are used to describe certain neighbourhoods — Greenbush, Beehive and Poplar Grove. None of these identities exist on any map.

Directions can drive one to distraction.

"You go past the old Ross place, where Eldon Weber lived before the barn burned," my chicken plucker once told me. "Then turn right at the new silo that the Crispin boy is building and drive past where the old Greenbush school was before they put up the white house where Mrs. Reid lived until she went into the nursing home. I'm the next lane to the south." It took almost as much time for me to find his farm as it did for him to pluck the darn chickens.

Unless your deed goes back to the time that the Crown granted it to your family, you do not live on your farm. If the person who owned your property had it for a few generations, then your farm will bear their name for your lifetime. If the person who owned your property only owned it briefly or (heaven forbid) it was owned by a numbered company, then your farm will be named after the person who owned it the longest before you did. You can put up signs galore. You can paint the barn turquoise and write "Brady Bunch Farms" in eight-foot-high purple letters. The locals will still tell you that you live on "the old Tilden place."

This is exacerbated by the fact that many people go by different names than those that appear on the mailbox, especially the men. I had a few of these nicknames explained to me in the pub.

Take a guy known as Spider. His real name is Thomas Noonan, but even when his mother gets formal she calls him Tim. He is also called Tim-Bob, because during the peak of the TV series *The Waltons* someone decided that he resembled the lanky character called John-Boy, but Tim-Bob sounded better. It was his gangly height that earned him Spider.

Rooney, who is actually Richard Young (even though everyone from his boss to his girlfriend call him Rick), earned his title because he has a tendency to whine in the tradition of *60 Minutes* television commentator Andy Rooney. The local disc jockey, Doug Kerr, has always been known as the Suds or, affectionately, Sudser. To the roads superintendent falls the title Pothole King, but if you want to point out a pothole to him, you have to ask for Demo. It seems after one particularly long night in a pub, he required a designated driver. However, before anyone could be designated, he managed to demolish a large quantity of other vehicle bumpers in the parking lot. Hence, Demo.

My neighbour Ken Houston pronounces his name "house-ton," But I named him Hooter because come haying time he starts hooting and hollering. It stuck. In return, he named my companion Moose, which automatically designates me Mrs. Moose. All and any names can be followed by the word "cat." I doubt that this has anything to do with the beat generation or "hep cats," but you end up having a beer at the tavern with the likes of Bob-cat, Tom-cat and Moose-cat.

There is no such thing as an unwed couple in the country. If a fellow parks his car in your driveway for three nights running and you attend at least one social gathering in his company, you might as well get hitched because explaining anything different just will not wash. If two men live together in any sort of relationship for a long period, they will end up being called "the bachelors." Young men who live together are likely to be called "the fellows." Two unrelated women who set up house are called "the girls," no matter how old they are. Sexual preference is rarely discussed outside of the privacy of the coffee shop, where everything and anything is reported, discussed, condemned or supported.

If you are new to the country, you can expect to be stared at, but not spoken to unless you say something first. This can be too much for some people. I had a painfully shy acquaintance who bought a big old house in town as a renovation project, but she left halfway through the job because she just could not take being stared at constantly. If she had told people who she was and what she was doing to the house, they might have stopped staring.

You can expect to be granted privacy in the country, but that won't stop people from finding out who you are. They just won't bug you.

Years ago, actors Michael Sarrazin and Jacqueline Bisset spent a month living with their friends Robert and Marlene Marklein in Egremont Township. Sarrazin had recently starred in the Academy Award-nominated film *They Shoot Horses Don't They*, and Bisset's film *The Deep* was playing at the Roxy Cinema in town. They were movie stars. When they strolled into the drugstore, they positively twinkled. No one in town so much as asked for an autograph. When Robert introduced Jackie to Bill the supermarket manager while they were waiting for some chicken breasts to be boned, all he said was "nice to meet you, ma'am." To this day, ask Bill and he can show you the exact spot in the store where he met Jacqueline Bisset and feigned indifference out of respect for her privacy.

Once you get used to the lingo and the lay of the land, the country is just another living landscape. The problem becomes one of translation. It is up to you to remember that if city friends are invited to dinner it means that they are coming for supper. Directions are best provided in map form, along with a full description of property and the number of mailboxes to pass before you get to the correct lane. You may get used to telling people that your place is the first on the left after the railway tracks but is impossible to find a farm that exists along the railway tracks now that the railway tracks don't exist any more.

In the end, you just have to go with the flow and all things will be revealed. One day you'll wake up with a nickname that you can't get rid of. And no matter how hard you try, you will never get an egg from a capon, but once a layer quits laying, she's headed for the stew pot no matter what time of day you decide to eat.

And every winter is bound to be a doozie.

A Labour of Love

ON LABOUR DAY, I like to turn the tables a bit and make the laziest guy on the farm do some work. On that Monday, the ram gets down to business.

It isn't much of a strain. After all, the guy only works two or three times a year for a maximum of about 30 days, and none of those are exactly what you would call manual labour.

In fact, the working conditions are a kind of macho ram's dream.

All the big fella has to do is make love to his flock of adoring ewes. He's a stud, plain and simple. Two hundred and fifty pounds of paternal genetics waiting to happen. Once he's completed his task, he can lie down in green pastures until the next season.

The terms of employment are, however, very strict — get the job done or face extinction. The odds are heavily stacked against the male of any species living a long life on any farm. Heck, you don't even need a rooster to get eggs from your hens.

On a dairy farm, only the most exceptional males will ever qualify as breeding bulls. And even those fortunate enough to qualify often end up never actually enjoying a romantic moment. Their seed is collected into sterile tubes that are divided into smaller units called "straws," which are used to artificially inseminate the great mothers of milk.

Beef bulls are tending to go the same route. Making the grade is rigorous. The best of the crop of purebred bull boys often end up on test station farms where they are evaluated for everything from how much weight they gain on an average day to the size of their breeding apparatus.

Size does count on the farm. For instance, I would never consider keeping even the most charming of runt ram lambs as flock sire. As they say in boxing, truth is in the "tale of the tape."

Years ago I was attending a sheep show and sale where the competition was fast and furious. One fellow in particular was promoting his ram as the best thing that ever walked on grass. And it was a pretty animal — washed white as snow, with shiny black hooves, a gleaming black face and a pedigree as long as a rack of lamb.

The sad truth came when the veterinarian who was inspecting all of the animals called for "the tape" and discovered that the fancy ram was a few critical centimetres shy of the scrotal circumference that makes or breaks a breeding ram.

The poor owner threw a woolly fit when he was told of the disqualifying characteristic.

Manhood and ramhood melded as one.

A recount was demanded. But the tale of the tape was just as damning the second time around.

"Nothing personal," the vet kept saying, as he backed away from the enraged owner who had worked himself into a stomping, red-faced, testosterone-fueled rage.

The undersized ram was led quietly from the building, while his charged-up owner required a three-person escort who were subject to a freewheeling range of expletives. It is one of the few times I have seen a shepherd truly lose it. And I never saw that shepherd or any of his sheep in the show ring again.

With some pride, I can report that my ram, Magnus, survived the tape. He is fit and handsome, and there's a gleam in his eye. On Labour Day Monday I will dress him in his breeding harness, a leather affair that holds a bright crayon marker at the front of his chest. Then he will be taken to the breeding field where the chosen ewes have been gathered.

From then on, it is up to him to do his job without supervision. The crayon is my only intrusion. Each time Magnus works his charms, it will leave its mark on the ewe. In a few weeks, the whole group of ladies will be sporting a red streak on their backsides.

I like to think there will be romance — and tender moments of baaing and cooing — but that is something only the sheep will know.

I will know if Magnus is the worker I think he is sometime late in January, probably during the halftime ceremony of the Super Bowl. From start to finish, it takes anywhere from 148 to 152 days to make a lamb. So I figure that one or two of the ewes who catch his eye on Labour Day will inevitably be giving birth as the last game of the football season plays out.

At least, that is what Magnus had better hope happens. Otherwise, he's out of a job and off with his head.

THREE STRIKES AND THE SUMMER IS OUT

SUMMER OFFICIALLY ENDS for me with the final game of the Slo-Pitch League. It is a game that is sure to happen long before the World Series gets underway, while the sumach bushes are still tinged with scarlet and the geese are gearing up for the flight south. It is also a "sure thing" because there will never be a baseball strike in the slo-pitch league. Millionaire baseball players and owners may think it is okay to huff and chew when they should be playing ball, but at diamonds in every rural town the boys and girls of summer have never stopped trying to whack the ball over the cow palace building.

When I was a kid I used to watch my six uncles play baseball on a dusty old diamond that didn't have any fancy lights for night games. The village bleachers would be packed with families. If a game went on past sunset, cars and trucks would scatter around the diamond and we would watch the finish of the game through a blaze of headlights. The crack of the bats, the whistle of the pitch, the endless moment of a fly ball dropping slowly from the sky, and my strapping big uncles charging from base to base in a swirl of dust — that's the real field of dreams.

Now I am not a baseball player. My one season of play ended when I ploughed into a first baseperson who had the specific gravity of a brick outhouse and injured my knee. Then a cow kicked the same knee, and I have been on the injury reserve list ever since.

I am a fan, and my team of choice is the UIC Flyers. The team was formed about a decade ago when most of the guys relied on the Unemployment Insurance Commission for their daily bread. Things change. Now they all have jobs and families, but they still don't have full baseball uniforms.

There is nothing fancy about small-town baseball. The Flyers wear T-shirts sponsored by their watering hole of choice, a construction company and a guy who kills lawn weeds. Instead of the usual player numbers, they decided every shirt should just have a Number One on it. of course, they all have baseball caps, which are worn backwards unless there is a brutal sun.

Baseball doesn't need to mean fast-ball. That's really a young person's game. Slo-pitch is a kind of genteel baseball, a sort of a signpost on the geriatric coast toward lawn bowling. Instead of blinding pitches, the ball is thrown underhand. There are no dramatic, belly-skinning slides into home plate — that would be too dirty and dangerous. Instead, runners just trot past the plate. At that rate, you can keep players going well into their 60s.

I knew of a team that called itself La Bats, and they thought they were hot stuff. They tried to stack the roster with youngsters and hard hitters, which earned them the nickname La Dorks. Slo-pitch is meant to be fun. When a team by the name of the Master Batters went to the finals one year and heard their name incorrectly pronounced as one word over the loud speakers, everyone was laughing except for their wives.

Each season there is one perfect game. One game in which everyone on the team plays like Robert Redford in *The Natural*. It's the kind of game where double-plays happen every other inning and home runs abound.

The fans go wild, and a sort of baseball-speak takes over the English language. A ball hit low to the ground, for instance, is a "worm burner." And a pitcher doesn't throw the ball, he "tosses the dark one." There is always one guy in the league who yammers non-stop through every game in an idiom that goes something like: "Have an eye, this is the one. The sticks are ready. The sticks are hot. Just give it a nice light poke. Touch a bit of green."

One year the UIC Flyers lost 14 games in a row, but they still managed to win the championship. They took this as an omen and promptly declared themselves World Champions.

A celebration was in order, and the team asked for permission to party for a weekend at my farm. Younger people might call this a "field party," but the Flyers took it one step further. For instance, I was somewhat surprised when a full-blown work crew appeared on the scene and spent a non-stop weekend erecting a 20-by-30 foot covered stage, complete with an electrical system capable of handling an eight-piece orchestra. They even installed an outhouse with a dandy crescent moon on the door.

On a Saturday afternoon, a steady stream of campers poured up the laneway with all manner of tents and trailers, kids and barbecues in tow. Someone rounded up a wagonload of picnic tables that were strewn in a clearing in front of the stage, and the decorating committee installed Christmas lights through the evergreens. It was a nippy evening, and everyone assembled down in front around a bonfire, while the second baseman acted as deejay, playing everything from Bob Dylan to Bob Wills.

It didn't take long for real musicians to appear. Country and western guitarists and Irish minstrels play slo-pitch. At one point, everything from a mandolin to a penny whistle were blended in harmony. Before supper was served, "Amazing Grace" was rendered in a bagpipe and saxophone duet. Then there was a talent show and the first baseman won with a mean display of break dancing. By the time I went to bed, the embers were cooling to the last strains of "Kumbaya."

The next morning, while the smell of bacon and eggs filled the air, the Flyer kids were playing baseball in the pasture. Shortstop Craig announced his engagement to Miss Ellie and the World Champion UIC

Flyers toasted them. I kept expecting Shoeless Joe Jackson to wander out of the cornfield.

By Sunday night, my fields were once again my own. Soon the empty stage was packed with hay for winter feeding. Summer had ended appropriately with a celebration of baseball.

Apple Annie in Eden

Sheep are curious creatures. If one member of the flock develops a particular interest in something, all of the others are sure to follow.

One fall a ewe, whom I now call Apple Annie, developed a passion for finding fallen fruit. After most of the apples had been picked from the rambling ancient trees in the small pasture outside my kitchen window, I let the flock roam through to find sweet windfalls in the afternoon.

Apple Annie decided the orchard was Eden. Every day at 2:30 p.m. she would stand at the orchard gate with an expression of anticipation as fervent as that of a 10-year-old waiting in line for a hockey star's autograph.

Naturally the rest of the flock saw her standing there, and they were curious. Soon the entire flock started joining her at the gate — baaing and shuffling — with visions of apples dancing in their small brains.

Annie led the charge of the wool brigade into the orchard. Keeping her nose close to the ground, she sniffed her way through the grasses to find the last apples of fall.

These were the runtiest of apples, smaller than a cueball but easy to crunch. Gluttonous cattle have been known to try gulping apples whole. As the story I heard goes, one poor cow managed to get a large fruit lodged in her throat just behind her windpipe. Her owner tried all sorts of methods and potions before calling a friend for advice. They ended up holding a plank against her backside and giving it a heck of a whack with a sledgehammer. Out popped the apple. A vision of that fiasco was lodged firmly in my mind as I watched the flock mindfully chewing their "finds."

A few good winds blew most of the straggling apples down with the last of the autumn leaves. While most of the sheep had the sense to retreat to the barn, Annie and a few of her faithful followers convinced themselves that foul weather simply meant an apple bonanza.

Snowflakes had fallen, but Apple Annie continued begging to enter the orchard. I humoured her, although her nose snuffle through the frosty grass was usually fruitless. One day I spotted her standing perfectly still under the oldest apple tree, looking at its great curled and gnarled boughs.

After an hour of watching her standing like a statue, I decided to find out what her problem was. Sure enough, swinging in the breeze from one of the top-most branches was an apple that would not fall.

Now I am no great marksman, and there are many healthy groundhogs on the farm who can attest to the poor shots that I have made. But for Annie I figured I could probably wing an apple. I took steady aim with my faithful .22, and the crack of the rifle sang out high above Annie's head.

The apple twirled on its stem and seemed to waft to the ground. Annie was on it in a flash, apple juice dripping from her jaws. If sheep can smile, she was grinning from ear to floppy ear.

GLASNOST CAN BE DUCKY

IT WAS A fine and sunny autumn day when we plucked Gorbachev.

Gorbachev Duck, that is.

I was just starting to batten down the barnyard hatches in preparation for winter, when I had a semi-frantic call from my friend Mia, a poet and shepherd who moved to the country about six years ago. Since I have been on the farm twice as long as she, Mia assumes I know a lot more about farm-type things than she does. So when she decided that Gorbachev was ready to become dinner, she called to request a hands-on demonstration of the delicate art of plucking a duck.

I have plucked my share of waterfowl, and the one thing that I have learned is that I would far rather buy a fully naked bird at my local supermarket. But Gorbachev, Mia's singular duck, had been grain-fed and deliberately raised for a feast. So we gathered in the woodshed and assembled the tools of the trade: an axe, a few sharpened knives, pails of various sizes and, of course, a hair dryer.

Mia's husband, Tom the Philosopher, fetched Gorbie from the barn. He was a fine big Muscovy duck with a kind of huge red wattle on his bill, which spread in a red patch over his white head and earned him his name.

I expect Tom and Mia had discussed the actual killing of Gorbachev from a variety of philosophical, poetic and moral aspects. Although I volunteered to do the deed and thus absolve them of guilt, Tom had obviously contemplated the awesomeness of the task at great length and determined that he should take responsibility for his duck in death as he had in life.

Once Gorbie was released from this veil of tears, the business of plucking began.

Mia provided a large bucket of warm water. The theory is that the water helps loosen the feathers. Getting a duck soaking wet is another matter. Ducks are virtually waterproof if you soak them head first. So we stuffed the duck in the pail tail first and swished him around until the water penetrated layers of feathers. A couple of tablespoons of laundry detergent helped to disperse the natural duck oils.

Then we put the wet duck on a table and six hands started to pluck. Feathers were flying and for the first five minutes we were going great guns. Half an hour later, no one was in that much of a hurry. A 12-pound duck packs a lot of feather. And under the feathers there is down — tiny fluff with an uncanny ability to fly directly up your nostrils as soon as it is plucked.

I tried to save the down from a half a dozen plucked geese. Many years ago I had *Harrowsmith* visions of creating my own duvet, but in the end there was not even enough for a whoopee cushion. Plucking gives you a lot of respect for feather pillows.

We were picking out pin feathers with tweezers when Tom decided he had to go to his study and memorize *The Critique of Pure Reason*.

I cleaned the inside of the duck, while Mia marvelled at the various entrails — brilliant coral lungs, a sleek and slippery liver and the hardened block of gizzard. She examined each organ like some kind of Greek oracle as I explained what it was. It turned into a sort of Duck Anatomy 101 session. Although I take the business of evisceration quite seriously, I did have to laugh when Mia gingerly touched the two almond-coloured, walnut-sized globes that I removed from the mid-section of the duck.

"These are remarkable — almost opalescent, so very delicate. I wonder what they are?" she exclaimed, cradling them gently in the palm of her hand.

As it happens, those were Gorbachev's testicles, which caused Mia to drop them very quickly.

Tom hung the duck from a beam in the root cellar while Mia and I proceeded to blow-dry Gorbachev and pluck the remaining downy feathers. It worked quite well. One year I tried covering the down with melted wax. Theoretically, it is supposed to harden and then it can be peeled off with all the down cleanly affixed. However, I ended up with a sort of duck candle.

The final step was singeing the bird. Underneath all of those feathers, ducks have a smattering of hair that has to be burned off. It just takes a flick of the Bic to come up with a totally bald duck.

It took about two hours to get Gorbie ready for the roast pan. I'm sure that he will make a fine feast. As I left, the look of the poet crossed Mia's face and she set off to compose a poem of grace for her Gorbachev dinner party. I wonder if there is a word that rhymes with glasnost?

PUMPKIN MOUNTAIN

IT MUST HAVE been a good year for pumpkins. At my local Co-op store, they gave them away with every tank of gas. Roadside stands were chock-a-block with pumpkins of all shapes and sizes. And then, of course, there was my neighbour Joy's manure pile, a veritable Pumpkin Mountain.

It is hard to imagine a manure pile as a thing of beauty. But last autumn it seems Joy and her girls made a batch of pumpkin pies for a church supper and deposited the pumpkin entrails outside the barn on Dad's front end loader, from whence they ended up atop the manure pile.

Then in the spring, the manure pile started to sprout. Hundreds of pumpkin seeds came to life in the warm compost of the two-storey-high pile. Soon there were vines cascading down the slopes. Great leafy jungle-type vines that seemed to grow overnight. It was a magical thing.

Somehow Joy convinced her husband to let the manure pile be for the summer, while we all watched and waited. Sure enough, pumpkin flowers appeared throughout the summer, big horns of yellow blossoms amid the dark green foliage.

The triumph of it all came in the autumn. A true mountain of pumpkins graced the barnyard — big ones, little ones, grumpy-looking ones and pudgy little round ones. It was the kind of sight that makes you just stand back and grin.

I don't know why, but there always seems to be something laughable about pumpkins — maybe it has to do with the concept of growing a vegetable that is bigger than one's head, but about the same shape.

Still, there is only so much you can do with a mountain of pumpkins. Joy and the girls harvested a huge batch. They hosed them down and had a pie-making bee. Then they stacked a jumble of them up at the end of the laneway along with corn stocks and a straw man dressed in Dad's old coveralls as a kind of display. But even that left dozens of homeless pumpkins to be dispersed around the neighbourhood.

I am not a big pumpkin pie fan, but my sheep just love the flesh of the big squash. So I loaded up a pickup truck full of pumpkins and took them home for the flock. For a month, I hauled four or five pumpkins into the pasture every few days. After scattering them around, I'd get out my axe.

The guinea fowl thought this was a great amusement. Five of them perched on the rail fence to watch me wander around whacking pumpkins to pieces. As each pumpkin split, they would squawk with delight and run like fiends to poke through the pumpkin pulp and gulp down the slippery seeds.

The sheep think pumpkins are just grand. They ran through the orchard gnawing and nibbling at the sweet orange flesh. The vitamin boost was good for them, and they surely enjoyed the change of menu.

My horses, on the other hand, have no pumpkin appreciation. They found the sheep's treat a rather stupid joke on my part. The only orange thing they find worthy is the carrot.

By late October, I had just about exhausted my pumpkin supply, and Joy's once joyful pumpkin mountain was relegated again to a plain old manure pile waiting to be spread on the fields. In the meantime I carved two big, old, grumpy-looking pumpkins into smiling, square-toothed wonders with lopsided eyes and triangle noses. They sit on cinder blocks on the front porch waiting to glow on Halloween night.

Chances are that I will be the only one to see them. Kids don't tend to trick or treat in the country, where pickings are few and far between. The best I can expect to see are a four- and six-year-old ghost and goblin team from down the road, who will make a quick stop before heading to town, where they can fill their bags in an hour by leaping from door to door.

Come the witching hour, I expect to be in bed. When I blow out the candles in the old jack-o-lanterns, I'll make a special wish. You see, I buried their bountiful seeds at the top of my old manure pile this year. And I hope the guinea fowl don't find them, because I'd really love to see a mountain of grumpy-looking pumpkins in my barnyard next year.

Winners, Losers and Hermaphrodites

FARMERS ARE A bit like gamblers. We tend to remember the wins rather than the losses. For example, I thought the hermaphrodite sheep was sure to end up as mutton. Instead, I ended up selling "it" for twice the price of a purebred breeding ewe! It was a glorious reversal of fortune, since economic success stories are all too rare on the farm.

The animal in question was one of a fall-born set of triplets. A little dumpling of a lamb, it always looked stout and square. I recorded the sex of the lamb as female. Obviously, I acted in haste, but there were not any telltale testicles to cause me to think the lamb was anything else. "She" grew at a tremendous rate and she came from a good family, so when it came time to decide which lambs would be keepers and which would end up fetching a fine Christmas price at the butcher's, I decided to keep her.

It was spring shearing time when the duplicitous nature of the lamb's sexuality reared its ugly head, so to speak. Underneath the winter wool it seems the lamb had been developing male apparatus, albeit quite small.

"Saw one like this entered in a fall fair once," said Judy the Shearer, who has seen just about every form of sheep and shepherdly quirk that exists. "This guy had entered a really big yearling ewe and everyone thought she was sure to be the top of the class. Then the judge ran his hand under her belly, and sure enough he found a surprise. I don't know who was more taken aback, the judge or the sheep."

I did some checking and found out that hermaphroditism occurs in sheep with about the same regularity as snow in June, but it does happen. The hermaphrodite sheep may have two sets of organs, but neither of them usually develops sufficiently to fulfill any particular function of reproduction. So it is really neither here nor there. I was stuck with an infertile sheep of questionable sexuality — too old to qualify as lamb to my trained palate, and too big an eater to keep as a curiosity.

Before I could decide what to do with the sexuality-challenged animal, a sheep breeder of some distinction scheduled an appointment to see the purebred stock I had for sale. I wanted the whole flock to make a good impression, so I hid "Hermie" (as I called "it") in a back pen behind a stack of straw. I did not want one mutant animal to put a potential purchaser off his cheque book.

The visit went well. My secret was never discovered. By the end of the day, I was helping the breeder load half-a-dozen lovely ewes and a top-of-the-line ram lamb into his trailer.

"Now all I have to do is find another 'it,'" he said, as he wrote me a solid cheque. "Mine finally died after 14 years and I sure could use another."

Two weeks earlier I wouldn't have had a clue what he was talking about, but now my interest was piqued. Sheepishly, I told him that I just happened to have an "it," but I had never considered selling "it."

"Sure you won't reconsider?" he asked. "I'll pay a good price for a new 'it.'"

It seems the dual sexuality of a hermaphrodite sheep enables an "it" to detect sheep that are cycling and ready to breed. The male component of the "it" apparently comes into play during the breeding season. When the testosterone kicks in, the "it" responds as though it were a bona fide ram. Fitted with a breeding harness, the hermaphrodite will dutifully mark ewes that are ready to breed. Thus forewarned, the good shepherd can then deliver the ready and willing females to the service of the "real" ram.

In a one-ram operation this would not seem to have much advantage. However, in a large purebred flock, knowing when a ewe cycles and directing her to the sire with the most complementary genetics is a big advantage. In a way, the process is the same for thoroughbred racehorses. A "teaser" stallion of indiscriminate breeding generally susses out the mare. Then he works himself into a frenzy determining precisely when conception is most likely to occur, only to have the job completed by pricier horse flesh. This must be particularly frustrating for the teaser stallion, but it would not faze a sheep like Hermie. The other advantage of an "it" is that when breeding season is over, the feminine aspect of the hermaphrodite returns. This incarnation is a more docile, manageable animal to work with than a strong-willed, potentially dangerous ram.

I had not intended to be cagey about selling Hermie so that I could drive a better bargain, but that is what I had unwittingly done. The breeder examined "it" from top to bottom and announced that "it" was exactly what he was looking for. My embarrassed reluctance only fueled his passion for full possession. With the cheque handsomely revised, Hermie left my barn to enjoy a long and leisurely life that would include total freedom of sexual preference. The breeder gave "it" a name: B.C.

"I name all my sheep after movie characters," he explained. "I just couldn't decide whether to call this one 'Bonnie' or 'Clyde.'" I have not bred a hermaphrodite sheep since. Years have passed, and I still double check the sex of the lambs from that particular genetic line. I guess that's the farmer in me — always looking for a loser who could turn out to be a winner.

A Hunting She Will Go

It is getting to be that time of year when a country girl's thoughts turn to guns.

The goose and duck hunting season has opened in my neck of the woods. You can always tell when it starts because people who normally tend their businesses closely sometimes disappear for days at a time. They always seem to be a few guys short at the lumberyard, and sick leaves rise dramatically at the factories in town. The Canadian Tire store usually runs out of shotgun shells.

Unlike my rural friends, I wasn't raised with guns. The only gun I had seen first-hand before coming to the farm was the revolver the police officer wore to my public school when he came to talk about Elmer the Safety Elephant. I subscribed to the Freudian notion that men who used guns were trying to extend their penises, and considered hunters to be a Neanderthal form of life, probably poorly endowed.

One thing country life has taught me is that an outsider shouldn't criticize blindly or try to impose alternative values before understanding the ones that exist already. Conventional wisdom boils down to two facts of life: having a gun in your possession is a serious business and being around guns without knowing how to handle one is just plain stupid.

I hated the notion of having a gun in the house, but you cannot use sweet persuasion to move groundhogs, and the holes they dig in the pastures where my sheep and horses cavort are leg-breaking deep. The country boys hunt groundhogs with .22.250-calibre rifles that blare like cannons. They use mushroom-head bullets that explode internally. As the saying goes, "They blow 'em up real good."

My decision to learn about guns was the culmination of a lot of things, including groundhogs. A pack of wild dogs ripped apart one of my sheep, leaving a tumble of entrails for me to find before breakfast. A rabid skunk bit one of my cows and led to her demise. Cantering along the edge of a hayfield next to ground-hog mounds made me wary.

And being alone made me feel vulnerable. During a full moon, I could hear neighbours who I'd been warned were "a bit slow" literally howling at the moon. One of them took to walking the road at night and leaving mash notes in my mailbox. One midnight, a man I barely knew arrived drunk on my doorstep demanding beer. Another drunken local showed up wanting to waltz in mid-afternoon. I felt a sense of the film *Deliverance* in the air, and with it, my own defencelessness. Not that you can use a gun to defend yourself in this country. The issue for me was more letting it be known that *this* woman living alone in the country wasn't about to let varmints of any sort overrun her property.

I called the cop shop and discovered there was no handy-dandy, one-day, all-you-ever-wanted-to-know-about-guns course, so I enrolled in a provincial hunter education program. This five-week, 15-hour course was conducted in the basement of a United Church. My fellow students consisted of 30 guys wearing Penzoil and STP T-shirts, as well as a handful of women who were the wives of hunters hoping to save their marriages.

We studied everything from the five different types of gun actions to the habitat of upland game birds. Some sessions were spent looking down the muzzle of guns and crossing imaginary fences safely, others included films with titles like *Shoot, Don't Shoot* and *Ducks at a Distance*.

The final test wasn't easy. There were 60 questions that covered topics ranging from the essential parts of a cartridge to the environmental ramifications of hunting. About 20 percent of my class flunked before they even got to the practical part of the exam.

The "practical" consists of handling guns and moving with guns under the watchful eye of a conservation officer named Sir, who asks a barrage of questions. He can ask you to do anything from loading a gun to unloading a gun to demonstrating all manner of gun carries. Then, out of the blue, he might ask the bag limit for black ducks on any given day. If your gun barrel wavers in the direction of anything human, you are simply asked to leave.

I came away a licensed hunter, with a code of ethics and a knowledge of guns that made me feel a whole lot safer. Word of my achievement spread like wildfire. While my city girlfriends teased me with nicknames like Bambo and Duckbo, the bag boy at the supermarket showed me a new respect and the town newspaper publisher clapped me on the back. I found out that one of the top trapshooters in the local sportsmen's association is a woman who works at the drugstore, and there is considerable respect for her ability. When men learn that another woman is learning to shoot they just wrinkle their brows and mumble something like "hope she leaves a deer for me."

That year, I hunted for the first time, going after the Canada geese that make annual predatory swoops on the local corn fields.

Don't get me wrong. I like geese. They are magnificent birds. But my cousin, who crops his land for a living, figures the annual migration of geese through his fields can cost him up to one quarter of his cash crops every year. This means his wife takes a night-shift job at a factory and he takes handyman jobs just to keep the kids in decent winter boots. So it is that I came to understand that shooting a few geese and scaring off the rest is something of a survival tactic. No wonder I have no trouble getting permission to hunt on my neighbour's land.

I fired three shots but nothing fell from the sky, so my hoard of wild goose recipes remain untested.

I probably will try again this year. My shotgun is cleaned and gleaming. I've done some target practise and reviewed all my safety lessons. One of these crisp autumn mornings a small group of us will don our camouflage gear and traipse off to the edge of the cornfield in our bright orange hats. By sunrise we will be laying low, sitting on tree stumps, some on one side of the field and some on the other.

We will hold perfectly still and watch the frost on the boughs of ancient apple trees dissolve as the sun comes through the clouds. In that enormous quiet of dawning we will hear the corn stalks creek and the sparrows start their morning twitter wars with the starlings and crows. Far in the distance we will hear the honking of geese, and as the sun crests, the leader of the flock will fly over on a reconnaissance mission.

Then we will blow our goose calls making odd squawks that will recall childhood memories of New Year's Eve blowers. The sound will drift over the brown-flowered heads of fence-line burdocks and purple thistles until the V-shaped flock of 200 Canada geese passes overhead so close that we'll hear the feathers beat against the din of their honking.

I might take aim and shoot, and I might not. The mere sight of me at that hour of the day in such ridiculous clothing should be enough to scare my neighbour's marauding geese away from his fields forever. Ultimately, just being there at the edge of a cornfield at dawn is enough of a trophy for me.

TALKING TURKEY

WHEN I SAY grace over the Thanksgiving turkey, I always add my own private thanks that I did not have to grow the confounded bird.

I tried raising my own turkeys a few years ago, but once was enough. I was placing my spring order for day-old chicks and I noticed that the hatchery was also selling baby turkeys, so I ordered a dozen. With a hundred or so chickens ranging around the farm, I figured that a few turkeys could not do much harm.

My pal, Henry the Chicken Farmer, happened by the day I was installing the fluffy yellow chicks and the gawky, bald-headed baby turkeys in their pen. He laughed, called me Pilgrim, and told me he gets a real good chuckle out of young idiots from the city who haven't got the sense to just buy a Butterball when they crave a feed of turkey.

Henry then proceeded to offer me a quick course in turkey maladies and idiosyncrasies, along with some plain language talk about what he calls "the stupidest bird ever created."

First off, I quarantined my turkey poults. It seems turkeys and chickens just do not mix, and turkeys can give chickens a deadly disease called Blackhead. That meant building a new turkey pen, at a cost of about six store-bought, table-ready birds.

Chickens have never impressed me as mental giants, but at least they have enough sense to eat and drink. I had to physically impel each baby turkey to the feed trough and provide the occasional refresher course in water drinking.

During the summer, the turkeys gobbled around in a pen next to the garden. They would flap their wings, but they weren't much for flying. About the best they could manage was a wild hopping gallop when they saw me coming with fresh carrot tops or corn cobs. All seemed right with the world, until we had a drenching rain.

The chickens were smart enough to run for the cover of their coop and perch on their roosts like sensible birds. The turkeys, however, stood in the middle of the field with their beaks upraised, swallowing the pouring rain. Two of them literally drowned themselves before I could herd them to safety. Another one had to take a spoonful of vodka before jump-starting to a sputtering revival.

While I was towel-drying the survivors, I began to wonder which of us had the smaller brain. Henry the Chicken Farmer told me he has seen flocks of 200 turkeys drown themselves in the rain. Great.

And turkeys are vicious. Chickens will occasionally rumble and rooster feathers will fly, but given enough space to range they tend to be fairly peaceable. The turkeys, however, literally pecked one of their own to death and tried to eat him!

"Cannibalism is just a phase they go through," advised Henry.

You would think that turkeys who could shred a fellow egg-mate into bits would be tough guys, but a few claps of thunder turned them into total wimps. They would cower in a corner, piling on top of each other, and I had to wade through and separate them before they suffocated each other. A woman gets to feel a bit addled when she rides out a lightning storm making soothing gobbling sounds to a bunch of terrified adolescent turkeys.

If you live with turkeys long enough, you finally reach a point where you start asking basic questions such as, "why do they exist?"

Consider the fact that the basic construction of a turkey is totally silly. The big white gobblers we devour at Thanksgiving are genetic hybrids of the original lean, dark-meated wild turkeys.

The fact is that not everyone wants a drumstick, so breeders have developed turkeys with a lot of breast meat. As a result, commercial turkeys cannot even reproduce without a helping hand. There is simply too much breast meat on a good breeding tom turkey for him to accomplish what nature intended, and the poor hen turkeys' legs were not designed to support heavy loads. So breeding hens must be artificially inseminated.

I found this out from my friend Susan, who spent one less than idyllic summer working as a "turkey jerker" at a big fowl breeding farm. Talk about a career opportunity. Ultimately, Susan became a blacksmith. She has strong arms.

The best time I ever had with my turkeys was stacking their plucked and vacuum-sealed torsos in the freezer. For once, they did not smell rude or gobble back at me.

From that day forward, I have stuck to raising chickens. When a turkey is called for, I do the simple thing. I make a pilgrimage to the supermarket and pluck a prime one out of the cooler.

KISS A PIG FOR A CAUSE

IF YOU WANT to raise money for anything in the country, you need to get the local bankers on your side. Not because they are pillars of the community or persons of great charity, but rather because they are generally and roundly despised.

Charitable groups, recreation committees, hospital boards and youth committees all suffer when farm commodity prices are low. The tightening of farmers' belts ripples through the community. Banks are generally the first to respond by reducing lines-of-credit, insisting on added security, or simply foreclosing.

So when a "dunking" game is featured at a fall fair, you can bet that the star attraction is going to be a banker. Dunking contraptions are fly-away chairs or bars set over large tanks of water. You pay a buck for a ball and try to hit the pie plate that releases the seating contraption and plops the subject into the water. Large crowds gather to observe this humiliation, and long lines form to risk a loonie on the chance of satisfaction.

When a banker is scheduled, some joker is almost certain to dump a few bags of ice into the tank to add to the "vig."

During periods of killing interest rates, whole baseball teams stand in line to dump the banker. If you get a hot-shot, never-miss pitcher at the front of the line, it can be splish-splash-banker-takes-a-bath time for two solid hours. Teenage boys may get a kick out of dumping the Dairy Princess, but anyone old enough to have applied for a loan waits for a banker.

I gather that this was not always the case. There was a time a few generations ago when some rural bank managers inspired certain veneration. The bank earned the trust of farmers, and cash that once lived under the mattress went into the bank. In those days a banker might live out a lifetime serving the same clients, but in these times knowing the client too intimately is considered a disadvantage. The unseen evil known as "head office" makes sure that bank managers change every few seasons. This allows the banks to remove any notion of consistency. It also supplies a steady flow of fresh fodder for the dunking tank.

Communities are always trying to figure out new ways to raise money. A few years back, the idea of the duck race took hold. This involves selling bright yellow rubber duckies and letting them loose on the stretch of river that runs through most towns. Then someone decided that teddy bear picnics could be a grabber, and soon Bear Days were popping up everywhere. Such themes are worked to death, until another genteel idea springs forth. They work but, without revenge on a banker as the finale, they are about as exciting as watching bubbles rise in pancake batter.

Bingo is a main staple of fund-raising. The most innovative variation on that theme is Cow Bingo. This involves a heifer and a controlled area that is divided into squares, which are sold by number. The heifer is fed and watered substantially, and let loose on the gridded plot. The game involves selecting the square where the first cow pie lands. Sometimes the judges have to wait for hours before they shout "bingo!" On the rare occasion when a banker is the winner, the local newspaper tries to run a picture of the winner beside the "deposit." Then, there is general praise for the acumen and aim of the heifer.

One contest that bankers always win is Kiss a Pig. In fact, if there is more than one financial institution in town, you can bet that those managers will place first, second and third, relative to their general foreclosure rate. For the price of a loonie, the populace is invited to nominate and vote for the local person they would most like to see kiss a pig. Tax collectors, police chiefs, school principals and dentists usually capture a fair share of the votes. But since there can be only one winner, it is the abused clients of the banks who dig the deepest.

"The nice thing about Rollo is that he doesn't care who he kisses," said the swineherd, who offered his prize boar to buss the people's choice. Bank managers have been known to apply for transfers when confronting Rollo. Let's hope that automated tellers never take control of the world.

HEDGEHOG FUTURES

I CALLED MY neighbour Rick the other day to find out how the great Minto Township hedgehog raising experiment was going. Every fall, it seems Rick tries out some new critters as on-going investment strategies. One year it was bronze-back turkeys, and another time it was African cats with super-long tails.

As you may have noticed, raising exotic species has become somewhat of a trend in the country. A farmer on a main highway close to where I live regularly stops traffic with his long-necked, puff-bodied llamas. And every summer, miniature horses are a big hit at the senior citizens' picnic. While "real" farmers have concentrated on building cows the size of a townhouse, those who dabble often end up channeling their efforts into Dexter cattle, a rare Irish breed that stands about waist-high.

Behind tall fences there are beefalo, buffalo and bambis chewing hay where dairy cows once roamed. These days, you can find everything from Vietnamese pot-bellied piglets to full-grown wild boars ranging in fields and barnyards. There is a whole contingency of bird raisers who are convinced that ostrich could be the Thanksgiving dinner of the future. I'm not sure what sort of stuffing you would use on an emu, but I know a woman who paid $9,000 for the privilege of trying to hatch some. of course, when I consider some of the "exotics" I have kept, I have to be the last one to say that there isn't a market somewhere for everything.

So when Rick announced he was getting into hedgehogs, I tried to nod politely.

"Gonna sell them to pet shops," he said.

It seemed almost logical. After all, if people are willing to keep ferrets on a leash, the market in hedge-hog futures could be a goldmine.

But something about hedgehogs bothered me.

So I went home and looked them up in the ency-clopedia. Sure enough, they were exactly what I thought they were. Funny-looking, rodent-type gaffers, covered with sharp spines that protrude nastily when the pointy-snouted beast is scared and curls into a pincushion. You could fit one into a lunch pail.

I'd only seen a hedgehog once in person, on a moonlit night in Denmark some 20 years ago. They are nocturnal creatures that spend their day hiding out, quite literally, under hedgerows.

The next time I saw Rick, I asked how the hedge-hogs were going.

"Great, just great. Got them set up in a terrarium in the living room," he said.

"But don't they sleep all day?" I asked cautiously.

Rick's a private sort of person, and in the country we just don't pry directly into private affairs all that much.

"Yeah, but they wake up around midnight and then they're really fun to watch," Rick told me. "That's why they'll make good pets for shift workers."

Logical, once again.

Rick himself had a night-shift job, so he was just waking up when most us were starting to dream. At that giddy hour, apparently the hedgehogs were merrily rooting around their terrarium, digging for earthworms and playfully nudging each other the way buddy hedgehogs do.

By November, I figured Mrs. Hedgehog might be about ready to have a litter, and I hoped to have a peek at what could be the pet-trend of the '90s.

Nope.

Rick had already taken his profit in the rising hedgehog market. He'd shipped the four-legged urchins to Alberta — where hedgehog fanciers are apparently clamouring for pets that go bump in the night.

THE GREAT MINTO COW HUNT

THERE IS NOTHING like a cow on the loose to turn grown men into frustrated children.

The other day, driving along the gravel roads on the outskirts of a small town, I observed such a phenomenon in action. Five men were chasing a dairy cow around the front lawn of a farmhouse in an attempt to move her back into the barnyard.

I pulled my truck up, knowing that a loose cow is the equivalent of a loose cannon and she could decide to bolt across the road at any given moment. True to form, old "Bossie" was soon joyfully kicking her heels sideways, throwing up stones like some bucking rodeo steer.

The men knew what they were doing. They fanned out and moved slowly, trying to surround the cow without alarming her. But something seems to snap in the mind of a cow when it realizes a taste of freedom. Even though she had probably been trained to head to the milk parlour morning and night along with the rest of the docile milking herd, in the outside world the cow became a maniac.

However, the calm containment method of herding was working — until the cow saw some laundry flapping on the line behind the house. She bolted through the blue jeans, running full-bore around the house via the clothesline and ending up beside the front porch draped in a flannelette sheet.

At this point an angry woman appeared on the porch, brandishing a broom. One firm shout from her scared the cow enough to send her ambling off to the barnyard, shedding the sheet in the autumn leaves.

Five men ran shouting and waving as they dashed to close the gate behind her. Then they perched on the fence looking at their captured quarry, no doubt having words about her parentage.

It reminded me of one of the reasons I don't keep cows anymore.

Years ago, I bought Hazel the Hereford and Lindy the Limousin from Henry the Chicken Farmer. Along with Hazel and Lindy came their calves, Herman and Heathcliffe, two funny-looking gaffers whose father had been a Highland bull, a pedigree that gave them long shaggy coats and the nubby beginnings of horns.

Henry drove his livestock truck into the pasture and I prepared to photograph the arrival of my first cows. I have pictures of the truck doors opening with the cows and calves wandering out. The rest of the pictures are of their backsides as they ran to the top of the field, jumped the fence and headed off over the neighbour's fields.

I didn't find my cows for three days.

A full-scale cow hunt ensued. All of the neighbours were on the lookout for the travelling foursome. Posses in pick-up trucks toured the gravel side-roads. The police were notified. The local country and western radio station carried a public affairs announcement about "four stray cattle beasts in Minto Township," and I got out the horse.

You can cover a lot of distance on horseback, and I rode from dawn till dusk. We jumped fences, forged creeks and interrupted many sunbathing groundhogs. After two days of tracking and finding tufts of shaggy hair on fence posts, I figured they were still somewhere in the area, which was small comfort to my saddle sores.

Phone calls were coming in from as far as 30 miles away, reporting possible sightings. Finally, a young couple from Toronto called to say they had enjoyed watching my cow family graze peacefully in the back field of their hobby farm near the highway for several days.

With the help of Henry the Chicken Farmer and the horse, we herded the renegades back on the truck and took them home, depositing them in a pasture with fences that were reinforced, and had a single strand of electrified wire around the top.

Hazel, as belligerent a cow as I have ever met, immediately headed for the fence, but one touch of her nose on the electric wire was enough to send her dancing back into the pasture. All of them had a go at sniffing the strange wire, and after a couple of high-

stepping bovine tangos, they determined the boundaries of their new home and settled into eating and
mooing and doing regular cow stuff.

I never trusted the cows after that. I could feel
them watching me every time I opened a gate. I could
tell by their sneaky cow faces that they were just biding
their time for one lax moment when they could once
again bolt their way to freedom and make a fool out of
me.

The Great Minto Cow Hunt made good conversa-
tion in the neighbourhood for months. I could not go
to an auction without someone chuckling and making
inquiries about the present address of my cows. The
only comfort came when I discovered that virtually
anyone who has ever had a cow has at least one tale of a
merry chase of hamburger on the hoof.

So when I drove away from the scene of the
escaped Holstein, I felt a certain camaraderie with the
five men perched on the barnyard gate. I knew that
once they retired to the kitchen for coffee, their stories
would start about cows that had escaped, and quite
possibly they would recall the three-day cow hunt in
Minto Township by "that lady with the sheep."

ELWOOD'S UFOS

THESE DAYS, ONE of the cheapest forms of entertainment in the country seems to be attending public meetings where land severance applications or zoning changes from agricultural to residential are hot topics of discussion. Public meetings are most often held in a township municipal office, where elected officials meet once a month to discuss burning issues such as where a drain should go and whether or not a dog catcher who has been convicted of unlawfully killing dogs should be re-hired. Anyone can attend such regular meetings, but the real fun is when a "public" meeting is called because there is bound to be controversy between the pro- and the anti-development forces.

And then, of course, there is the question of what's going to happen to the UFOs if all this development takes place.

Almost every month there is a notice in my mailbox informing me that someone nearby is applying to sever a lot or two off their farm. This raises all kinds of environmental questions about land use planning, sewage percolation rates, the right to farm and the right of farmers to make a buck by selling off a bit of real estate.

All things considered, my neighbour, Elwood, is more concerned about the effect all this development is going to have on the UFOs that rely on his private lake as a water refueling centre.

Elwood is the kind of aggressive old-timer who will sit in a wooden chair and rub the arms and claim that he can tell you how old the tree was. When a man claims to know the age of trees by touch, you are best just to nod in agreement. That's also the best response to give regarding discussions of the UFO water refueling issue.

A few years ago, a group of neighbours got together and formed an association with the unwieldy title of Concerned Citizens for the Pike Lake Area and the Environs. We get involved in local issues like preserving agricultural land, maintaining wetlands and generally keeping a watchful eye on anything that threatens to pollute our water or our way of life.

We added a concern for the UFO situation after a discussion about the wisdom of placing an 18-unit subdivision on a provincially significant wetland, which just happens to be next door to Elwood's private lake.

The Indians used to call Elwood's 15-acre lake Spirit Lake and later the pioneers called it Ghost Lake. It has always had an aura of mystery. The lake is set back from the roadway and you could drive by the fieldstone house Elwood built by hand and never know that paradise was only a few hundred yards away.

I first visited the lake when I was about five years old, on an excursion with friends of my parents who were friends of Elwood's. From Scarborough, it seemed to me that we drove for hours to get to the "wilderness."

There is a trail cut through the bush where pheasants and grouse hide. At the lake, a rustic cottage sits perched at the water's edge, and I remember holding my fishing pole out the window and reeling in fish that Elwood cooked as fast as we could catch them.

When I discovered that Elwood was my neighbour after moving to this neck of the woods almost a generation ago, it brought back all kinds of good memories.

Elwood's lake is unchanged; the trees just keep getting bigger. Nearby, progress has taken a certain toll. On a lake a few hundred acres away there is a huge trailer park. Nature just doesn't look right with 400 mobile homes racked up side by side. No self-respecting pheasant would want to nest amid that accumulation of barbecues, and all those septic tanks can make the air smell distinctly unnatural.

Elwood, however, has guarded the pristine nature of his lake. He has pet names for the catfish that live under the dock, and he claims they come when he calls. One year he announced that there were five bullfrogs missing at the lake. It seems he also counts his bullfrogs every spring.

Eccentricities aside, this was the first any of us had heard about Elwood giving the UFOs permission to stock up on water from his pond.

"All I can say is that if they build houses, the extraterrestrials won't be coming back," declared Elwood, during a discussion of the effect of development on waterfowl nesting sites. "They don't like a lot of people around watching their spaceships," said Elwood, leaning back into an 102-year-old maple chair.

According to Elwood, ET and his buddies have been bringing their frisbee-shaped spacecraft to his property for over 40 years. They suck water out of his lake and carry on with their journey. Makes me wonder if they didn't make a mistake once and suck out five bullfrogs while they were at it.

"If they can't get water here in privacy, I guess they'll just die," advised Elwood. "They won't go near a lake with a subdivision on it, no sir. They won't even come near while the trailer campers are around in the summer."

We all quizzed Elwood about the logic of what he was saying, but he refused to budge.

If Elwood is right, this could be as important as discovering the Lost City of Atlantis next to the Dome Stadium. It could certainly create quite a stir at a public meeting.

If it went to a judicial hearing, it could be even more interesting. Imagine trying to explain to a judge that, sewage percolation rates aside, a development should not proceed because it will disturb the aliens' watering hole in Minto Township.

I'm convinced.

CASKET LIDS AND OTHER FOUND TREASURES

PACK-RATISM IS RAMPANT in rural areas. One of my neighbours collects old doors. Another keeps a trailer full of abandoned windows of all sizes. If I ever need an anvil, there's a retired Irishman two townships away who keeps a shed full of them, for reasons known only to him.

Every farm I have ever visited has a designated area for "stuff." In a shed or a corner of the hay mow or stacked behind the barn, there's always a pile of wood left over from some project, various roll ends of different sizes of wire and snow-fencing, windows, odd-sized doors and baskets of nuts and bolts picked up at an auction that might come in handy some day.

I inherited just such a pile of debris when I moved to my farm. At first it just looked like a mess, but when I needed an instant panel to divide a pen, there were always a few pieces of lumber that could be sawed and whacked into shape. Old window panes made perfect cold frames for spring vegetables and odd pieces of barn board were made into shelves, saddle racks and chicken perches.

The farm has provided me with the impetus to develop skills I never thought I would have. One year I put a new floor in the chicken coop. It still surprises me that I know what to do with a mitre board. When I conquered the use of a drill, I put screws into everything. None of this is art, mind you, but it does have a lot to do with form and function.

My neighbour Alex tells about his great-grandfather building a stable entirely out of wood. The only things that weren't wood were the door hinges. Those were made of leather. Alex's grandfather swore that all he needed to make a log cabin was an axe. The handle was used as a measure and the width of the axe head was used as the depth of the dove-tail on the end of the logs to be fitted at the corners. In those days, they didn't have a pile of "stuff" to rely on.

Left to my own devices, I have been known to build some pretty funny looking things out of scraps of wood. My first A-frame chicken house was rather lopsided, but it served its purpose.

When you are forced to improvise for economy's sake, a lot of things can be recycled. An old shower curtain stapled to the windward side of my pump house wall has stopped the wind and rain for 10 years now. One of these days it will be replaced by proper insulation and an interior wall — but that could be five years hence. In the meantime, every time I see the shower curtain holding firm, I take a peculiar pride.

The township dump has proved somewhat of a treasure trove. I have come up with discarded twin bed frames that make ideal lightweight lambing pens. Buckets, barrels, leftover steel siding and fence-roll ends that have all been another person's junk have found a useful purpose in my enterprise.

When I needed a few small pieces of quality wood for some kitchen cupboards, I let it be known throughout the neighbourhood. Sure enough, an offer presented itself. You can imagine my surprise when I found myself in an empty hay loft that was stacked with beautiful pieces of oak and cherry wood. The only thing was that they were discarded casket lids.

"Too good to waste," said the owner, Elmer, who is a practical man.

Somehow I could not countenance the notion of having coffins as kitchen cabinets.

My friend Clare ended up with a real boondoggle on his hands when his dad died and left him a farm that had hundreds of ancient vehicles simply left hither and yon. Just when he thought he had found everything, Clare would look over the crest of hill and find another cache of rotting metal on wheels. There was everything from Model-Ts to early motorized milk trucks. Some of the rusting heaps from the '30s still had the original gangster bullet-holes in the bodywork. What seemed at first like a disastrous removal and disposal proposition turned into a gigantic antique car and car parts auction that brought buyers from all over North America.

The best I have been able to find on my farm is an ancient plough hidden under wild grapevines, and a pile of old car licence plates amid some smashed whisky bottles that somehow ended up in the middle of a swampy patch of forest.

Apparently, our forbears were not always the most ecologically minded citizens. Under aged mounds of moss, I have unearthed everything from rotting tin cans to green-glass mason jars that someone felt comfortable ditching in a cedar bush clearing. Of course, some of this historic debris now qualifies as "antique." I can perch etched-glass medicine bottles, defunct milk bottles and oddly shaped pop bottles in front of a window and the sun streams through their coloured glass and hand-hewn shapes, beautifully belying their garbage-pile origins.

Every fall I am tempted to cart the "stuff" I have been hoarding to the dump. But somehow I know that I would miss it in the spring when I need the odd piece of two-by-four to shore something up, or a sliver of plywood to cover the wear in a certain step. So far I have eschewed casket lids, but there's always next year.

THE UNPREDICTABILITY OF A FARM WEEKEND

ON A COOL country weekend at the farm, what could be better than a cosy fire crackling, while a simmering stew bubbles and the smell of fresh-baked bread fills the air?

Sounds good to me. I sure wish someone would come over and set things up just like that for me.

When you actually *live* on a farm, weekends just can't all be the "over-stuffed plaid sofa, window-box herb garden, long, quiet communes with a book" lifestyle that you see in magazines. Weekends are not necessarily reserved for finishing that tranquil needle-point or creating some marvelous handhewn bird feeder. Nothing is that predictable.

Take the dogs on a rambling hike through the woods and you are just as likely to find yourself mired knee-deep in bog or burdocks as you are to interrupt a small herd of deer peacefully wading in a stream.

Plan to attend an auction that is fully stocked with antique crockery, hand-tatted lace and oodles of those quirky old rug beaters that can positively define a room, and — just as you intend to leave — the phone will ring with a neighbour in crisis requiring an extra hand to steady a horse that's having trouble giving birth.

These are things that happen. But when you try to warn city friends that a "weekend at the farm" means anything that goes on at a farm will keep going on — well, they just think you're kidding. The funny thing is that once a city person arrives in a country state of mind, they think that just about anything that happens is quite marvelous.

For instance, I remember the day that Herf got out.

"Herf" was only a few days old. I bought him at an auction, a mistake I tried not to make — but there he was, a little Hereford bull calf hiding off in a corner away from the larger, black-and-white Holsteins.

He was such a little guy, no doubt a classic runt or the weaker half of a set of twins. He seemed to cower in the corner as though he wanted to hide from the auctioneer's gavel. When I caught his eye he looked so forlorn, so motherless.

My maternal instincts found me stopping for a bag of calf milk replacer powder while I drove home with the hapless Herf in the back of the truck bawling his brains out.

We arrived at about the same time as the guests. Herf descended from the truck like a good little orphan and we took the baby boy to the barn and gave him his first bottle.

The city folk loved that. The red-and-white calf, so soft and trusting, nuzzling and thrusting away at the big bottle with warm milk supplement in it. He lay down in his straw and gave a great burp.

"Terrific," said the city folk. "We've done some farming already. Now where's lunch?"

We were well fed and ready for the mandatory walk in the woods when one of the urbanites decided to check on young Herf. In doing so, the city person made a crucial mistake and left the door open. Out of the barn in a flash, what had once been a sad-eyed, motherless bull became a frisky, mooing little butt-head. Herf wanted to play. Off he ran, with five folks in Eddie Bauer footwear — and me in my Wellington boots — giving chase.

Now you can't chase a cow, no matter how small. They just don't respond well. We would all have done much better to stop in our tracks and leave the poor, confused Herf to stand stock still and consider where his next bottle was coming from. But I could only convince my urban friends of this when they had reached a state of exhaustion after criss-crossing a 50-acre field like errant Pac-Men, while Herf bobbed and bucked ahead of them.

Finally, they retired when I promised to make them raisin-and-cheese scones and herbal tea flavoured from the window-box garden.

Herf showed up on the front lawn by the time we had finished. Two urbanites proceeded to charge at him with love in their hearts and a big hug in mind. But cows — no matter how little — have a privacy zone. Just like people on a subway, they like to think that some of the space they occupy is their own.

Herf's privacy zone involved not being hugged around the neck. He bolted. And again, five sets of Eddie Bauer boots and one set of Wellies set off in pursuit.

This time we stalked the little dickens. He was mooing for more milk and feeling forlorn. So we fanned out around him, crunched into commando poses, and moving ever so slowly, each one of us mimicked his mournful, Munchkin moo.

One of the ironies of life in the technology age is that every time you should have a video camera, you are part of the action.

As we funneled the little Hereford back toward the safety and warmth of the barn, I watched a heavy-duty mutual fund manager hide behind a gate post making soprano mooing sounds. His buddy, an expert in Egyptology, balanced the scene with an alto moo from behind a lilac bush. Shadowing them were assorted wives, lovers and children, all mooing intensely in an effort to make Herf feel as though he was part of a herd.

Heavy, wet snow and freezing rain began falling just as the diminutive Hereford entered the barn. Someone thought he was a bit wet, so I discovered the whole lot of urban cowboys massaging the baby bovine with my best bath towels when I got back with the warm bottle.

By the time Herf had sucked the whole thing dry, we were ready to repair to a crackling fire that I had managed to light, and a bubbling stew that I had managed to thaw in the microwave and transfer to suitable antique crockery. One of the guests had brought a basketful of fresh-baked breads.

As it turned out, we had a wonderful evening of needlepoint instruction and bird watching discussion — but who could have predicted that?

Winter

THE HAIR DRYER — MY
INDISPENSABLE FARM TOOL

WHEN I FIRST left the family home, twentysomething years ago, my father gave me a hug, a hammer and a multi-head screwdriver. My mother offered the same gesture of affection along with an electric kettle and a hair dryer.

I was on my own, and my family had prepared me with tools and appliances to cope with the world at large.

Today, after a decade of urban life and more than a dozen years on the farm, those implements (albeit slightly updated) remain indispensable. I keep them all together in my barn where they enjoy constant use.

The hammer and screwdriver have been joined by all manner of other small tools and corresponding sizes of screws, bolts and nails. I am still not what you would call "handy" with them, but I have come a long way from my first attempts to hang a picture. The kettle is good for a comforting cup of tea during winter lambing, and for heating up cold buckets of water during difficult animal births or making a warm mash for the horses.

It's the hair dryer that confounds almost everyone who visits my sheep barn. But of all my family tools it is the one I find most indispensable.

I first discovered the many applications of a hair dryer in the barn in the middle of a particularly active party, which included a house-full of guests. Naturally, there was a blizzard featuring a minus 20 windchill factor, but being a good shepherd I thought it prudent to take a quick barn tour before partying hardy. I had checked to see that the mangers were full and the hatches were battened down, when I heard a small high-pitched bleat from the back of the barn. There I found a ewe milling about a frost-encrusted newborn lamb.

Lambs were not scheduled to arrive so soon, but I vaguely remembered one early August day when the old ram had built up enough steam to leap the fence and join the ladies. Obviously, I did not catch him before at least one unscheduled romantic interlude occurred.

I tried rubbing Frosty the Snow Lamb with straw, but I could feel that he had already taken a powerful chilling. My trusty kettle was frozen solid, so a hot water bath was half an hour away. As quick as I could, I set him and his mother up in a portable pen with a heat lamp and I dashed back to the house through the swirling snow.

My guests were swinging by this time. As I slipped inside via the mud room, it occurred to me that they had not even missed me. I sashayed into the bathroom and stuffed the hair dryer casually into one pocket and a hand towel into the other. My guests were having such a good time that they didn't even pause to question a hostess departing their midst with a small appliance protruding from one hip and bathroom linen from the other.

Back at the barn, the heat lamp was casting a warming glow and the ewe was licking the lamb to stimulate it. All the right things were happening, except now the frosted lamb was glazed with ice.

That's when I started blasting away with my trusty hair dryer, moving it in slow circles and rubbing the towel over the lamb. In about 10 minutes Frosty was dry, warm and eager to stand up and find the faucet of life. I gave the ewe some molasses water, warmed from the finally-thawed kettle, daubed Frosty's umbilical cord with iodine and left them to get acquainted as ewe and lamb have done so well for thousands of years.

When I rejoined the party, no one even noticed the mild scent of *eau de sheep* on their smiling hostess.

Since then, the hair dryer has enjoyed its own peg on the barn wall. It has warmed countless lambs, thawed water pipes and pumps, and even blown-dry a few baby turkeys who were too stupid to come in out of the rain.

So frankly, when I visit a barn that doesn't have a hair dryer, I wonder what tools and appliances that farmer left home with.

Just a Passing Windstorm

On the farm lots of things happen that you tend not to discuss at the dining room table. I do not mean blood and guts stuff or digestion-inhibiting economic stuff — I just mean normal, biological, animal, vegetable and mineral stuff.

For instance, every so often I will cut the string off a bale of hay and find a dead snake that got stuck in the alfalfa as it passed through the baler.

Occasionally, rain water will somehow manage to seep into a barley bin and cause a fermenting process that turns it into the kind of mush that breweries distill. It sure stinks before it becomes beer.

While pigeons may create problems in urban areas when they unwittingly fertilize window ledges, farm animals also "go" where they live and the droppings of a half-ton horse are far more evident. Animals do not ask for permission and they are not shy about nature's call.

What brings me to this is a weekend visit by my Toronto lawyer, his wife, and their children. It seems that the children, aged three and six years, had never been closer to farm animals than a television screen. As the visit progressed, I began to suspect that the same was true of the adults.

Although I always tell guests to dress casually for the farm and bring some old clothes if they want to feel comfortable in the barn, the allure of a "country" weekend seems to prompt urban folk to dress like British gentry rather than Canadian farmers. Fortunately, I have a stock of Wellington boots in various sizes for visitors, and the extremely active three-year-old male child was delighted to put on extra layers of socks so he could wear a bigger-sized boot.

There is this great thing that I do for city folk that drives them out of their minds. Long ago I developed a whistle call, based on the call of the killdeer. It is almost as haunting as a loon's cry.

From the empty barnyard I make my mournful whistle, and in the distance you can see the sheep and horses pull their heads up from the feeders in the snowy pastures and the next instant they are running joyfully toward the barn. City folks would not know it, but the animals come running because they are gluttons and they know their arrival at the barn means they will get a treat.

For my lawyer friend and his family, it seemed like some magical scene to watch the snow fly as the two palominos galloped in with their tails flying, while the sheep trailed after like so many white blips on a computer screen.

Horses neigh and the kids scream. Sheep baa and

the kids scream again. Geese honk and ducks quack, chickens cluck and fly off to their roosts.

This I am used to. These are sounds I love.

But as fate would have it, at that exact moment of country frenzy, good old Ken "the Hooter" decided to roll up the lane on his tractor to deposit a big round bale of hay for the assorted livestock.

Hay deliveries drive my animals wild. Apparently tractors have the same effect on three-year-old male children from Toronto. The six-year-old female child clasped her hands to her ear muffs, finding the tractor noise quite impossible to deal with along with the rest of the racket.

"Hooter" made a suitable display of jockeying the tractor around the yard and slam-dunking the huge bale into a feeder. In reality he is a normal-sized man, but something about captaining a tractor allows him to masquerade in a larger persona. Shouting above the din, he proceeded to regale my guests with the challenges a man who has "been on the farm for 35 years" experiences trying to help a novice like me feed animals. "Hooter" left in a veil of snowflakes. The three-year-old thought he was a superhero.

By this time the animals were really revved up and they commenced doing what animals do when they are mildly excited. The sheep urinated, squatting neatly in no particular order. The horses entered into a magnificent display of spirited trotting, snorting and bucking which was accompanied by sporadic flatulence.

The little girl, who had obviously been conditioned to appreciate certain social graces, was appalled by the scene confronting her. Her brother, on the other hand, was thrilled to observe natural processes that television had failed to convey.

"Tooter, tooter," cried the young lad as the horses ran off to the back pasture farting in stereo.

I saw mother and daughter feeding a ewe some grain from a pail. The sheep stood back and chewed thoughtfully while they stroked her head. I cringed when I saw her stumpy tail raise for an emission. "Mom, I think the sheep just fluffied," said the girl, turning her head delicately.

I am sure that the parents were relieved when I suggested we retire to the kitchen for hot chocolate.

Dinner presented a few challenging moments. The three-year-old insisted on practising all of the farm animal sounds he had learned. His sister rolled her eyes and the parents shook their heads.

When I tell Ken that animals "tooter" and "fluffy" at the sight of him on the tractor, I can guarantee there will be a whole lot of hooting going on.

Santa Claus is Coming to Town

Somewhere in a huge warehouse in Toronto busy gnomes spend months getting ready for the Santa Claus parade. Precision marching bands drill for hours practising those old familiar tunes, and the search goes out to find persons unknown to dress up as clowns that can walk on their hands for the entire parade route.

But the world doesn't stop or start in Toronto, and neither do Santa Claus parades.

In storage sheds and machinery shops all over the rural countryside, Santa Claus parade stuff happens at a furious pace. I know because I've been called upon to donate some old chicken wire and a bag of wool for a top secret project that I suspect involves some sort of snowman.

Every year "Grandpa" Bill, who lives alone on Sideroad One, spends months working with a dedicated crew on the float to end all floats. Early in December, it will roll down Main Street with a variety of other home-made concoctions pulled by tractors and pick-up trucks and teams of horses in jingle bell harnesses.

Anybody can enter small-town parades — and whole families do just that. You can bet that in some hay loft in the vicinity, a few generations are collaborating on transforming a hay wagon into a thing of beauty that will feature everyone from great-grandmother to the latest grandchild in a warmth of evergreen boughs and toboggans decorated with big red ribbons.

And somebody is sure to come up with a big old St. Bernard or Newfoundland dog, sporting a red plastic nose and flannelette reindeer ears.

Last year three police cruisers and four fire trucks made it into the parade. And there are always a few antique tractors decorated with flashing lights, and an assembly of classic old cars carrying folks dressed up like something out of Charles Dickens's *A Christmas Carol*. School bands and pipe bands join in the chorus, and mini-majorettes twirl their stuff in the frosty night air. The Kinsmen, the Lions, the Oddfellows and the Women's Institute all join in to create some sort of tribute to Christmas.

The clowns may not walk on their hands, but they do shake hands — and if you look real close you might just find that the person behind the greasepaint is anyone from your plumber to your chiropractor. Candies are tossed from each passing float, and kids scramble and squeal with delight.

If it sounds unsophisticated, it isn't.

Just consider what Grandpa Bill and company have to go through to make it to the parade on time.

First comes the concept. One year the parade theme was "Christmas is for Kids," and it worked so well that the parade committee decided to stick with it.

The hay wagon route is too mundane for Bill. The float he works on involves the developmentally challenged, so he likes to make the float itself a challenge — complete with lights, music and moving mechanical parts.

Last year this involved life-size, dancing marionettes. Another year it was skaters rotating on a turntable; the year before that, a toy tower that spun around. Accomplishing this involves a lot of mechanical ingenuity, not to mention power generators and batteries.

This year Bill and crew are launching an aircraft float. The wings are welded out of scrap metal from an old grain bin and the hull is crafted from a discarded water-heater tank. The plane rocks and rolls courtesy of the hydraulics from a gadget that normally moves bales of hay into barns, and the nose propeller spins courtesy of a 12-volt battery. The "pilot" even gets to ride in comfort, on the padded seat of an ancient riding lawnmower.

After six men mount this assemblage on a trailer, the lights are carefully strung. Although it will stretch the budget, the plan this year is for "chasing lights" that zap around in sequence, giving a psychedelic effect while the speakers blare out Burl Ives singing "Have a Holly Jolly Christmas."

In the cockpit, some brave soul dressed as Charlie Brown's dog Snoopy will be dipping and diving and tossing out lollipops. Who knows, at the end of the parade they may win a prize. At the very least, they will get their picture in the local newspaper.

While a million people may see Toronto's Santa Claus parade, only a few hundred will line the Main Street in town to catch the spirit and wave to Santa as he winds up the parade in a flurry of "Ho-ho-hos."

Frankly, I don't think little kids see much difference. And for the bigger kids, there is always the fun of watching your local butcher dressed up like a jack-in-the box, or your bank manager portraying the back end of a reindeer.

Those huge floats may fill the downtown streets with glitter and glam to draw the mongrel hordes directly into the prime shopping districts. But the sight of a full team of Percheron horses prancing in their jingle bells and pulling a wagonload of kids posing in the nativity scene does a lot more to fill me with Christmas spirit.

TREE THIEVES BEWARE —
PALAMINO ON PATROL

SOMETIME SOON THE dogs and the horses and I will make the annual trek through the evergreens in search of the perfect Christmas tree. We will try to wait for a sunny day, with a few snowflakes falling and the kind of crisp snow that crunches underfoot.

I have a 20-acre field filled with thousands of evergreens that range from me-high to over two storeys tall. So it can take half a day to find the perfect conifer — the one that fills the living room and scrapes the ceiling so that the star on top bends sideways.

I take red ribbons with me to mark eligible trees. When it boils down to two or three, the horse and I make a few passes around each one, looking for bare spots and making judgements.

I cut my tree with a hand saw. Using a chain saw just would not seem fair to the tree or the tradition, and it might spook the rabbits. With a rope tied to the tree and anchored to the western saddle, old Lady and

I will drag the tree home, with the dogs chasing behind.

If it sounds like something out of Currier and Ives, frankly it is.

My tree will not be the only one to leave the field. Although I am not in the Christmas tree business, my neighbours, their friends, the local hockey team and a few church elders will all be driving up the lane with their saws and their toboggans and their kids to take a walk in the woods and find their "perfect tree."

When I am not around, I leave instructions on the front door. These are simple things like "cut your tree close to the ground, close the gate when you leave and have a Merry Christmas." Just below that I tack an envelope for donations so that I can keep replanting.

It warms the heart to come home from a day of shopping and find an envelope filled with money, along with little notes of thanks and the occasional crayon drawing of last year's Christmas tree from a child.

Then there is the problem of the tree thieves.

Tree thieves do not respect signs. They do not pause to think about the damage they do to fences or the damage they do to trees. With thousands to choose from, it does not make much sense to scale a 20-foot tree only to lop off the top six feet — but I have seen it done.

It is not as though the tree thieves can't afford a tree from me — I am easy to negotiate with around Christmas. The local Food Bank knows that they have free access, no questions asked. I get so pink and squishy with the emotion of the season that I have even been known to cut and deliver for shut-ins.

But for the tree thieves in my neck of the woods, stealing a tree is also tradition.

I had this "tradition" explained to me in the local pub where all things are revealed, eventually.

"Don't ya know a tree is no good unless you steal it," a local golf course manager explained to me. He apparently had been stealing my trees for years and thought the trespass was a great game.

So I started the "tree patrol." I think the horse likes it more than I do. At random times of a weekend I slip on the bridle and we bareback to the fence-line, scattering pheasants as we canter.

The tree thieves are definitely surprised to be accosted in mid-hatchet-job by a mad woman on a charging palomino. I get all kinds of lame excuses like "I didn't know anyone owned this place" and "My friend said it was okay, his brother did this last year" and "We just thought we would take a look, but we found this one and liked it a lot. Who do I pay?"

It is Christmas after all, so I don't have the heart to call the authorities. Also, I have found that the first thing tree thieves do when confronted is reach for their wallet.

I enjoy knowing that Christmas trees from my farm are part of family festivities all over the township. The memories help in the spring when reforestation begins.

Still, the best part comes just before Christmas when the Food Bank gets a donation accumulated from the tree thieves.

It is enough to make a palomino smile.

WHAT MY TRUE LOVE
HATCHED FOR ME

ACCORDING TO THE song, on the third day of Christmas my true love should have given to me "three French hens," but instead he came up with three West African guinea hens that celebrated the season by chirping away under a heat lamp in the basement.

The week-old balls of brownish fluff and squawk look like a cross between a chicken and a pheasant. They run around their pen like mad, cocking their heads to catch a side view of the world and singing together at the oddest hours of the day or night.

The guineas in the basement came to be because "True Lover" found a nest of guinea eggs hidden in the brush near a cluster of cedar bushes during a mild-weather patch in November. No one knows why my few guinea hens decided to go broody and lay a clutch of eggs when frost was threatening, but they did.

The hens were not sitting on the eggs, just sort of laying them and hanging around them and wandering off. There were six brown speckled eggs in the nest when we found them. Having no idea how long they had been exposed to the elements, my inclination was to leave them be or throw them away. But my true love would have nothing to do with that. He fetched the incubator and placed the little eggs tenderly in its care.

Guinea eggs are smaller than regular chicken eggs, but they take a few days longer to hatch. By the time the prescribed 28 days had elapsed, the man in my life seemed to be spending half of his day peering through the glass-topped incubator for signs of life.

"Number three is rocking," he announced with glee. But I put it down to too much time wishfully thinking that an egg would hatch.

"Number five is peeping," he advised me a few minutes later. But I put that down to the chronic squeak in the floor boards.

Not to say that eggs don't rock and chicks don't peep before they actually hatch. They do. Sometimes, before a chick hatches out of the egg or even makes the first nick in the side of the shell to let you know that it's going to hatch, you can actually hear the little birds peeping inside their shells. And while the chick is pushing and poking to find the way out of the egg, it does often set the egg into a kind of rock-and-roll motion.

Just in case he was not a victim of a cruel imagination, we moved the eggs to a hatching tray.

Not half an hour later, the first baby guinea popped out of its egg, splitting the shell into two neat little pieces. Within an hour, two more had joined it and they were drying off nicely in the incubator, peeping like mad to find out what life is like beyond the egg.

I always feel some moment of tragedy when I take a chick out from the incubator. Here is a newborn thing with all the natural expectations of being mothered. But instead of downy feathers to hide under and the cooing of a mother hen to comfort it, a big human hand scoops it up and plops it in some wood shavings with some water and some food and a bright light over its tiny head. Other similarly confused chicks soon join the first hatchling, and they start to figure out basic things like eating and drinking together. But they have no role model to follow, just a big hand that intrudes on their space now and then to replenish their bowls and a big featherless face that looks at them through plexiglass and makes cooing sounds that don't sound at all like a maternal fowl.

The miracle of the Christmas guineas is that they hatched at all. Somehow, despite their fickle mothers and the vagaries of nature that should have stopped them dead in the yolk, they found a mentor who believed in them — a father hen, if you will.

The little dickens doubled in size in just a week, and developed tufts of feathers on their wings and tails. While their parents have dark grey feathers flecked with pearl-coloured spots and funny sort of purple helmets instead of feathers on their head, the baby guineas, who are called "keets," take at least a month before they begin to look like the birds they will become.

My true love, of course, is spectacularly thrilled with his little ones.

When he pokes his burly hand into their warm little brooding box, they crowd around it and poke him with their inquisitive beaks. He has hung a straw doll ornament intended for the Christmas tree in their nest area so they have something to play with. He shreds lettuce leaves into fine strips to make sure they get all of the vitamins they need. And instead of cooing at them, he makes appropriate guinea fowl sounds, which amount to a sort of sporadic, high-pitched repetition of the word "buckwheat."

Now I am on the look-out. After the three West African guinea fowl, it wouldn't surprise me to see a partridge take roost in the old pear tree.

CHRISTMAS ANGELS

FROM WHERE I sit, it looks like a white Christmas and I could not be happier. All of the hustle and bustle and shopping and tree trimming are done. In the country, we tend to get everything done one shopping day before Christmas Eve, because you never know when a blizzard is going to sock you in and close the roads.

The farm really does look like Christmas. At this time of year, I know once and for all why I painted the barns red and green. Even the sheep are decorated with shades of red and green across their rumps.

While it may look as though they have been designer imprinted for the season, the fact is that the red and green marks simply indicate that they have been bred by the ram. He sports a red crayon on his breeding harness chest plate that rubs off on each ewe as she is bred. Halfway through the breeding cycle, I change the colour to green.

The sheep look quite jolly actually. Of course, the horses are now wearing red and green halters. After chasing the biggest goose around the manure pile several times, the cat now sports a red collar, complete with jingle bells.

Who knows, maybe this sentimental penchant for dressing up animals at Christmas has something to do with a childhood spent in suburban Scarborough, where my parents foisted red ribbons on the cats and dogs and goldfish bowls at Christmas. It just makes me laugh.

While I was doing the last minute shopping for cranberries and whipping cream and cognac, I added extra carrots and apples to my shopping cart. On Christmas Eve, I will chop them up and toss them with pails of oats mixed with warm molasses. Around midnight, I will head out to the barn.

The animals will no doubt be sleeping when I tune the barn radio into Christmas carols. They won't understand why I'm waking them up, or why they have been roused for such a feast. Once they have eaten, they will settle back down and let me wander through the crowd, petting their noses, while the horses nuzzle me with frosty breath.

I will lean on the manger, jingle my sheep bells and let the emotion of the season wash over me in this most private of settings. Animals do not care if you get tears in your eyes, they nuzzle you anyway.

I will think about my family and Christmases past. I will think about the Christmas my dad and I built a model Brontosaurus, and I will think about the Christmas I had cancer.

I will think about all of the kids I have seen at Christmas and I will think about my long-departed grandparents who left me their memories and their recipes.

It is funny the things the mind flashes on. The baby lambs in the spring bouncing around like silly putty animals. The sweet corn from the garden. The goose hatching a dozen fuzzy goslings. The puppy trying to make friends with the barn cats. The horse trying to make friends with a skunk.

I will recall the sunny day we spent baling hay. I will think about the laughing and forget about the sore back as I celebrate the rewards of all the work that translates into the security and tranquillity of a warm barn on Christmas Eve.

I will think about an old lady I know who is missing her family from her nursing home bed, and my friends whose baby died, and the family I know who are losing their farm. I will let myself weep for them and ask, as they ask, Why?

And I will think about how blessed and lucky I am.

It is not a maudlin ritual, just one that seems to happen every year.

Once I have had it all out with myself, and everyone who needs patting is patted, I will close the barn door. On Christmas Eve the barn radio plays carols all night, and hang the hydro bill.

As I walk back to the house, with the carols softly ringing and the smell of the wood-burning stove inviting me to join my mate beside the Christmas tree for a cup of eggnog before Santa comes, I will find an untrod spot in the snow.

Then I will lie down in my snowsuit and do what I have done ever since I can remember on Christmas Eve. I will wave my arms and legs and make an angel in the snow.

Merry Christmas.

ALL SKUNK'S EVE

WHEN I WAS a kid my parents would get dressed up on New Year's Eve and go to a big party somewhere that kids could not go to. I'd stay home with the babysitter and my little brother and sister and I would try to stay awake until midnight, when Guy Lombardo and His Royal Canadian orchestra would play "Auld Lang Syne" from some glittering ballroom in New York City. I would always imagine that my parents were dancing at Mr. Lombardo's party, and that someday I would do the same thing.

In my dreams. But New Year's Eve on the farm has its own peculiar delights. I've had lambs born on New Year's Eves in the middle of blizzards, and one year the hydro went out for three hours, so instead of raucous music blaring, we greeted the New Year to the crackle of an ancient transistor radio and blew our little whistles by candlelight.

And then there was the New Year's I remember only as "The Eve of the Skunk."

It happened not too many years ago. I was getting ready to visit neighbours three farms away to celebrate with their family — maybe play a few hands of cards and tell a few tall tales. Nothing splashy. Nothing that needed a party dress or a fancy hairdo, but I do try to make it a rule to wear high heels on New Year's Eve, just so that I don't get out of practice. Also, I find that if you wear high heels on New Year's Eve, you can rely on gravity to tell you when you've tippled too much because you start to wobble in those darn things.

I was just set to leave, when I decided to let the dogs out for their constitutional. After five minutes, they had not returned. After 15, I knew something was amiss.

When I finally heard the familiar scratch at the door, one whiff told me they had found a skunk.

The larger, furrier dog had somehow managed to evade the black-striped beast, but my little dog — my house puppy, my wrinkled black Chinese shar-pei, Diva, who loves to lick my face and leap all over me — was suffering from a direct hit.

I slammed the door, whipped off my high heels and called the neighbours to explain I would be a tad late. No need to mention the skunk-sprayed dog.

Big Stella the Akita could have easily spent the night in the barn. In fact she often chooses to stay with her sheep. But the victim in this case was short-haired and spoiled rotten. Even closing the barn door in the face of the darling Diva dog is enough to set her into a baleful mourn.

When you greet a dog that is covered in skunk juice, the first issue of concern becomes containment, because nothing rubs off a dog easier than the fragrant oil of skunk. I quickly ran to the bottom drawer of a cupboard that holds a cluster of old clothing that's too badly damaged to donate to anyone.

Suitably attired, I dug the dog crate out of the basement rubble and lured the stinking Diva into it with a lamb-burger meatball that was supposed to have been part of my New Year's buffet contribution.

Diva did not take kindly to this entrapment, but I figured it was a better solution that having to de-skunk my entire household.

When I showed up at the nearest Becker's store looking like yesterday's hobo and buying out the entire stock of six cans of tomato juice, the fresh-faced young woman behind the counter said, "Gee that must be quite a recipe you're making."

A man who was carrying a bag of ice cubes offered his own opinion, saying, "Looks like someone's having a Bloody Mary party tonight."

But behind him there was a woman carrying a jug of eggnog who had "been there, seen it, done it" written on her face — "Skunk" was all she said.

"Dog got it," was my cryptic response. Profound communication is often the most succinct.

Fairly quickly, the other folks in the store caught the downwind scent of me, no doubt the consequence of hustling the dog into its temporary cage. It is amazing how the smell of skunk can permeate an entire Becker's store in the space of two minutes even after a minor contact.

Back home in the mud room, I proceeded to remove anything that I did not want to have ending up smelling of skunk. This included ambient clothes and boots, as well as snowshoes, an ancient toboggan and a misplaced garden rake. I mixed half of my tomato juice with warm water and coaxed the stinking dog into a large plastic tub, while a space heater tried to keep pace with the freezing temperatures outside.

De-skunking is an unsavoury art unto itself. Once the poor dog had abandoned herself to the inevitability of being bathed, I got into the swing of moistening her thoroughly with ladles of warm tomato juice. The theory is that some acid in the tomato juice neutralizes the skunk juice, but that takes time and more than one ladling.

After 10 minutes of ladling, Diva dog decided she'd had just about enough to suit her. She did what dogs will do — braced herself and gave a mighty shake — sending skunk-stink-laden tomato juice all over the mud room — and all over her impatient handler.

Three more tins of tomato juice and a few shakes later, we both repaired to the in-house shower for a well-deserved shampoo and rinse. By 11:30 p.m. we were both blown dry. The faint odour of wet dog, skunk and baby shampoo still clung to the air. Just in case I missed a few spots, I sprayed myself with flowery cologne. Then on went the New Year's Eve clothes and, of course, the high heels.

I arrived at the neighbours' just in time for the final countdown. Then there came a tap on my shoulder.

"Guess there's no point in offering you a Bloody Mary," said a low, familiar male voice.

Sure enough, the man buying ice at the Becker's store turned out to be my neighbour's brother-in-law. The woman next to him, another vaguely familiar face, offered me a glass of eggnog. Everyone at the party had heard the story about the lady in rags at the Becker's store who was buying gallons of tomato juice because a skunk had sprayed her dog.

Soon people were whacking me on the back so hard that I was tottering on my high heels before I'd even tippled. In the country, everybody has a dog-versus-skunk story to share.

Somewhere, I thought, there is a glittering party happening. Women in long dresses are dancing with elegant men and drinking champagne out of crystal glasses. In my dreams.

Maximum Blue Jay

Country living is definitely for the birds. And I mean that literally.

I have been feeding the birds for years — starting with one battered birdfeeder and expanding to five that vary from rustic barn-style imitations to high-tech, plexi-glass models and home-made suet holders.

The feeders are scattered throughout the bare branches of a huge lilac bush right outside the living room window, and the display of activity is non-stop. There is no set feeding schedule. The birds just come and go from dawn till dusk.

No doubt about it, the birds have figured me for a mark. Every spring I plant rows of sunflowers that grow to great nodding heights. I have yet to harvest any seeds, however, because the birds always beat me to it. Once the sunflowers are plucked, I begin to rely on the feed mill for a variety of seeds, and by mid-winter the birds are generally up to 40 kilograms per month.

Which brings me to my concern about a bird I have come to know as "Maximum Blue Jay."

This bountiful bird lives in the cedar and birch trees near a small marsh. I suspect that the only exercise he takes is the short flight to and from the feeder. Considering his paunch, I am sometimes surprised he can render himself airborne after gorging on sunflower seeds. Once I watched Maxi try to take a brief stopover on the upper branches of a craggy old apple tree, but the bough bent under his weight, causing great hysteria among the resting sparrows.

None of the other birds are overly plump. The chickadees who play and eat constantly seem to stay roundly sleek and the nuthatches are still trim enough to perch sideways on a branch without falling prey to gravity.

Finches, juncos, wrens, cowbirds and grosbeaks all visit the feeders at various times in their migrations. A variety of woodpeckers cavort on the suet balls. One year a robin startled me in February. It is only Maximum Blue Jay who finds it difficult to take a seat on the sunflower seed feeder and enjoy a mannerly meal. Lately his girth has become such a problem for the bird that he simply pauses to tip sunflower seeds on the ground where he plops down to eat in comfort. Frankly, I think Maxi is becoming an embarrassment even to his brother and sister blue jays.

Since they are relatively large birds and feisty by nature, the jays generally take control of the feeders when they swoop in to feed, relegating the smaller species to eat tiny seeds until their departure. The jays particularly enjoy scattering the more timid cardinals. However, Maximum Blue Jay has a tendency to ignore the other birds and concentrate on eating while they defend the territory.

Regulating feed in farm animals is a relatively simple thing to do. If a few ewes bulk up beyond a reasonable level, I can isolate them and cut back on their grain just enough so that they return to a healthy level of fitness. If I want a good plump chicken, two or three weeks of additional corn works wonders. But there just doesn't seem to be any way to work Weight Watchers on a wild bird that is determined to empty the trough.

Perhaps Maxi is the first wave of a strain of mutant wild birds, the off-spring of generations of feathered friends that have grown accustomed to the comfort of full feeders in winter. If that is indeed the case, it should be no time before my feeders spawn eggplant-sized chickadees and beefsteak buntings. I might have to reinforce the old lilac bush and add platforms to the feeders.

This may be the beginning of a trend. If Maximum Blue Jay claims a mate this spring, it could be the start of something much bigger.

I should notify the feed mill in advance. Ultimately, there may just be an emerging marketplace for sunflower seed "Lite."

ALWAYS OVERESTIMATE THE INTELLIGENCE OF SHEEP

WHEN I WENT to the University of Guelph to study sheep raising, one of the first things the instructor told the class was to always overestimate the intelligence of sheep.

He was right.

Today, as I braved a snowstorm to pile forks full of hay into the outdoor feeders, I found one ewe standing quietly inside one of the feeders.

How the sheep got herself in there I do not know. The feeders are four feet tall and meticulously designed to allow only the head of the sheep to enter the feeder. But there she was, and all I had to do was check the tattoo in her ear to confirm that one-year-old Gertrude had reached new heights of ruminant lunacy.

You would think that if she got into a feeder by herself, she ought to be able to get out. Not so.

Gertrude could not budge even when the rest of the flock was being fed grain which will generally make a sheep contort itself into extremely odd postures just for a nibble.

Under normal circumstances, I should have been able to just gently tip the feeder over on its side and send her gamboling off. However, the feeder was lodged in ice.

I would estimate that Gertrude has got about 60 pounds on me, but that didn't stop me from leaping into the octagonal feeder and trying to lift her over front feet first. I could get her front legs poised at the edge. But, when it came to hoisting her rump, Gertrude responded by collapsing her hind end like a full sack of wool at my ankles.

I reasoned that she must have bounded into the feeder with a running start. Getting out would require some form of staircase.

Operating on this theory, I tried to squash a bale of hay into the feeder to give her the height she needed to step to freedom.

Wrong. The bale could not squeeze in beside Gertrude and leave her any space. To complicate matters, the addition of hay to the feeder attracted other sheep who decided they should eat over, around and above the enclosed Gertrude. I managed to rescue the bale of hay, but not my toque, which Gertrude immediately decided to use as a foot warmer.

I tried levering the feeder loose with my trusty crowbar. After 15 minutes of bench-pressing the ice-encrusted feeder full of Gertrude, I felt it shift. Triumphant, I raised the crowbar above my head and let out a whoop to no one in particular.

This attracted the notice of the old ram, who has — for all intents and purposes — been fairly passive. But there's always a first time.

Out of the corner of my eye, I saw him charging. I had just enough time to dive un-toqued head first into the feeder with Gertrude. When you find yourself trapped in a hay feeder with a belligerent ram circling you and an immovable ewe standing with one foot in your hat and the other on your foot, the only thing to do is scream internally. No point in exciting the situation more than it already is. Once the ram lost interest, I literally crept out of the feeder and sidestepped my way to the closest fence.

It was time to involve technology.

I pulled up the truck, turned the lights on and cranked up a rowdy Hank Williams Jr. tape. The impact of this was enough to cause even the ram to back off as I leapt over the fence with a hook and a logging chain to tie onto the Gertrude-bound feeder. Scrambling back over the fence, I tied the chain to the bumper and put all four wheels into a slow reverse.

Through the flying snow I watched the feeder shift and, ever so gently, tip over despite Gertrude's attempts to counterbalance it.

So there was the feeder, tipped on its side. Such is the intelligence level of sheep that, instead of backing out to freedom, Gertrude was joined in the sideways feeder by another sheep with an identical I.Q. After a few blasts on the truck horn, they finally wandered out together.

As I disassembled my chains and fished my cap out of the feeder, I really had to wonder whether the intelligence of the shepherd is something that should not also be overestimated.

Wainscoting of Many Colours

There must have been a big sale on green paint sometime during the past century. Not deep forest green or velvety emerald green, but rather a dull cross between minty and putrid green.

At least that is one of the many shades of paint I discovered when I spent one winter stripping the wainscoting and wood trim in the kitchen of my old farmhouse.

Two townships away, the same shade of green showed up when a friend did some renovating. Just about everyone I have ever talked to about the original colours they discovered after buying a Victorian country home has some recollection of stripping or painting over this exasperating shade of green.

My house was in pretty good shape when I found it. Nothing that a few gallons of white paint couldn't cure temporarily while the basic necessities of sheep farming were attended to. So while many of my urban friends were concentrating their efforts on installing jacuzzis and Italian kitchens, I was working on fence lines and sheep sheds.

I am glad that I did not make any sudden changes to the old house. Living in it for a while gave me a chance to appreciate its past. It was built sometime in the 1880s with the yellow bricks that were the pride of a long-departed brickyard a few kilometres away. After I'd learned something about the families who had lived here, the children who were born here and the lively euchre games that had taken place in the parlour, the house came to remind me of a canvas on which other people had been designing, painting and wallpapering for a century before I arrived.

Any tinkering I do within these walls will end up being a message of some sort for future occupants. The marks I make on the house, just like the job of husbandry I make of the fields around it, become a part of a transformation that involves the history of all of us who have lived here.

This hefty, if somewhat sentimental, responsibility does not preoccupy my when I select new paint for a bedroom. However, there are elements of sincere craftsmanship that have gone into the old house and I want to maintain that integrity.

It was the integrity of the house that I had in mind one snowy day when I started to strip the kitchen wainscoting. In my experience these sorts of projects tend to start out small, and then take on a monstrous, never-ending quality. I found a tin of stripper and decided to find out what was underneath the dark brown paint around a door frame.

I uncovered faded yellow paint and some sort of cream-coloured paint before arriving at the dreaded green, but finally the wood was bare. It was a beautiful buttery oak, along with mixtures of other softer woods that had all grown in local woodlots over 100 ago.

The stripping chore took an entire winter, progressing inch by inch. It was a rubber-glove job that saw many pairs of gloves dissolve into gummy masses from the chemical stripper. All manner of tools were involved, including a kitchen sugar spoon that proved to be the perfect size to scrape between wainscoting boards.

You don't have to be a brain surgeon to strip wood. There is a certain skill in retaining the natural patina and texture of the wood without leaving it dry and raw, but other than that, simple patience and dogged determination seem to be all that is required. The greatest reward is living with the results.

So I was fairly taken aback when an interior designer acquaintance from the big city schmoozed into my kitchen one fine day and pronounced it to be a room "with a lot of potential."

Along with modern laminated cupboards and halogen light fixtures that look like aircraft, the designer envisioned "pickling the wood trim black to tie the whole room together."

At that point, I could easily have tied the designer up and installed him in a vat of brine.

As long as I am the custodian of this house, it will be proud of its age and happy to reflect its history without a lot of cosmetic surgery. The wainscoting will remain as naked as the trees from which it hailed. And for the sake of future generations, I will never buy green paint on sale.

THE PUMP HOUSE WARS

AS I GRABBED my pick axe and handsaw and went out into a blizzard to do my chores, I realized that maybe farming in winter does mean I am a few pickles short of a jar.

While city folks battle brown-grey slush in the downtown streets, I often find that just getting to the barn means leaping through thigh-high snow drifts.

One energetic, albeit "mature" Scottish shepherd friend has set up a kind of winter hazard fence line to guide him to and from his barn in blinding snow. He spaces the poles at intervals and each one is decorated with orange reflecting tape. If he takes three snowshoe steps without seeing a pole, he knows he's off track. The man is positively canny.

I try not to tread off the beaten track myself when snow is swirling. I have heard too many tales about pioneer days and even more recent times when a simple amble up an icy, snowed-in laneway led to disaster.

There are some chores that simply cannot wait for the weather to break — feeding and watering livestock, for example. Unfortunately, ice often freezes the edges of the big round bales of hay that are intended to allow the sheep to feed freely and provide some convenience for me.

This leaves me in the inconvenient position of having to bash the frozen bale with my pick axe and rip away the outer core of hay with my trusty hack saw. Sometimes it gets pretty frustrating. As soon as I have axed and sawed a bale open, the eager sheep descend. Making a quick exit comes close to scaling a Matterhorn of snow and wool.

Just when I manage to get everyone fed, the water pump generally freezes. At this point I have been known to pull my snow-covered toque over my face in the hope that what is obviously a bad dream will soon be over.

This year, the annual water freeze-up came after the chores and after supper. I discovered it as I prepared for a long hot soaking of tired muscles before bed. Oops, no water.

I have learned to keep a few gallons of water in the basement for just such occasions. While they boil on the stove, I clamber into my damp snowsuit and assemble assorted flashlights for the dreaded trip to the pump house, 150 long yards across a snow-drifted wilderness.

The pump house is a quaint little barn-shaped structure perched over a well and the pump is six feet down in a styrofoam-lined hole. Every winter I promise to install a staircase, but every spring I forget about it. An old crate is my only step into the pump hole.

After years of experience, I know that the trouble generally lies in a little rubber hose called the venturi tube, which must be massaged with hot water. It usually takes a few jugs before the pump clicks in, by which time a damp snowsuit can start to seize up. Getting out of the pump hole in a frozen snowsuit is an almost arthritic exercise.

Then there is a mad dash back to the house to make sure that the water is flowing. Air gets trapped in the line and it takes a few spurts and burps for it to work its way through to the taps. When the water begins to flow freely, the sight and the sound are mesmerizing. It's cheap entertainment, and it fills my heart with gladness.

After one particularly grueling pump house war, a girlfriend from the big city called me as I was thawing out by the fire. The poor darling had endured a dreadful day in the city streets and the road salt had fairly ruined a fine new pair of suede boots.

"I had to call you, because I just know that you are out there in the country having a great time, with your feet up by the fire and those darling dogs curled at your feet," she said. "I wish I could be there."

"Absolutely right," I told her. "There's no life like it." Then one of the big furry dogs shook wet snow all over me.

TRAINING TAFFY LOVELY

I HAD ONE of the errant dogs out on a leash the other day in an attempt to update long-forgotten dog obedience lessons. A passing Mennonite family pulled up their buggy to watch our antics from the roadway.

I have been known to pull up my truck to watch a Mennonite barn building or observe them in the fields with their horse-drawn ploughs, so I guess it shouldn't surprise me that they might also take the opportunity to observe the curious ways a former city person has of interpreting rural life.

In fact, I suspect it was the same buggy that paused a few years ago to watch me walking the piglet up and down the lane one frosty day. I hope they think that I have finally come to my senses and decided to train dogs instead of pigs.

The pig in question was only a few months old. A pink little girl pig named Taffy Lovely. She came to live with me to learn proper manners. It was nothing my life experience could have prepared me for.

When I lived in Toronto, the closest I ever managed to come to actual livestock was to observe the occasional chicken that tried to make a desperate escape from the late-lamented Stork's Poultry Market on Queen Street West. My altruistic '80s move to the country changed all that. I figured that I could manage raising a few sheep to break the solitude of a writerly lifestyle. After all, sheep are smaller than cattle, they do not kick or scratch and they only have front teeth on their lower jaw, so they cannot bite. What could be so difficult?

Soon I was adding chickens of my own. But I have always tried to keep the assorted livestock confined to their pastures and barn. This piglet was going to live with me, in my space, in the parlour where the Irish ghost of pioneer Tommy Noonan still holds euchre parties. It was all highly undignified.

Taffy was to become a "star." At least, she was to be used as a promotional pig for an entertainment magazine for swine breeders called *Playboar*, which was intent on entering the U.S. marketplace.

I had known the magazine's publisher, Tom Hagey, for quite some time. I was working as the editor of the "People" section of *Maclean's* magazine, when Hagey wandered into the offices one day wearing a pig nose and demanding to see "someone in authority." I'd just returned from an interview with Engelbert Humperdinck, so I guess the receptionist decided I could handle this guy.

My career has always been guided by the intervention of unique talents, and Hagey proved no exception.

After I became the first editor to abandon a national newsmagazine in favour of sheep, *Playboar* invited me to freelance as its resident book reviewer of the Miss Piggy tomes, and as feature satirical writer on subjects such as "Hog Air Ballooning" and "Hogtoberfest."

So when the notion of training a promotional pig occurred, naturally I was called. After all, what does a shepherd have to do in the off-season except train a pig?

Without a bunch of newborn lambs to tend, or crops to harvest or hay to stack, the "off-season" is something I've learned to look forward to. But the challenge of playing Miss Manners to a sow was irresistible.

My pig-training instructions were quite clear. Taffy had to learn to walk gracefully on a leash tethered to a pink body halter. She had to enjoy being petted and respond favourably to having her picture taken. Tricks were not out of the question.

I was assured that the generally sociable nature of pigs would see young Taffy Lovely literally begging to sit on my lap and snuggle within a few days.

This was not correct information.

The pig was moved into a rubber-matted pen in my parlour. I was assured that the intelligence of pigs was such that any piglet could be easily house-broken in several hours.

This was also not correct information.

Taffy confused my lap with a lavatory.

In the space of a very long week, I learned that a lot of things I had been told about pigs were totally untrue. At least, in the case of Taffy Lovely, stereotypes did not apply. She was nobody's Arnold Ziffle.

Taffy did not appreciate her comfy parlour pen. She vigorously applied herself to destroying it and she abused her squeaky toys mercilessly. Her idea of fun was to knock over her water bowl and squeal madly at two a.m.

She did not like to eat her pig chow while being held. In the lexicon of *Wayne's World*, she preferred to "hurl chunks." I tried coaxing her into proper etiquette with carrot sticks and slivered apples. Pig that she was, she quickly learned that emitting a deafening scream produced such tidbits to shut her up. In that regard, she was a quick study.

While training a dog involves making it fun for the dog to obey, training a hog as bull-headed as Taffy Lovely turned into a war of wits. Her halter, which was the same variety some parents use to tether agreeable toddlers, sent Taffy into hysterics. Asking her to walk calmly at my side rooted her miniature sow feet firmly to the ground.

After two weeks of trying, I was forced to admit that my best attempts at pig-training were a dismal failure and I had created a monstrous porcine brat.

Taffy was whisked off to complete her training with a "professional."

Within a few weeks, she was virtually performing cartwheels and smiling her pig smile on cue. By the time she arrived by plane for her debut in Chicago, she had flight attendants cuddling her and bringing her apples.

There was a full moon, and from the sofa I could watch the wild rabbits grazing on the fallen sunflower seeds underneath the bird feeder next to the satellite dish. I tuned in *P.M. Magazine* to watch "my pig" on American television.

The cameras were rolling as she emerged from a limousine and toddled elegantly along a red carpet.

A star was born.

Taffy and her publisher were interviewed in their hotel suite. Hagey wore his trademark pig nose and she wore a lavender garter. Taffy oinked contentedly on his lap when the microphones turned her way.

But I knew that pig well enough to see a certain glimmer in her little pig eyes. Sure enough, Taffy still thought a lap was a lavatory.

EVERYBODY GETS THE FEVER

AROUND THE MIDDLE of winter, the fever generally strikes. Cabin fever that is.

I don't recall it happening when I lived in the city, where I could call a taxi to take me to the airport on a moment's notice, or stroll into a cinema and have an instant choice of movie gratification, or dial a pizza when the cupboard was bare.

Life is different in the country, even when you've got your fax and your modem working, and all the folks on the Home Shopping Network want to be your friend.

There are days when the roads are quite simply closed. Days when the only external sounds you hear are the cackles of blue jays, the thunder of faraway snowmobiles and the insistent baaing, mooing, neighing and crowing of livestock waiting to be fed.

There is splendour in such isolation, but too much of anything can make anyone go a bit loopy.

Even my stoic Mennonite neighbours get cabin fever.

The other day I was driving along a snow-covered road when I noticed some strange tracks at the roadside. I discovered the contraption responsible for them was a horse-drawn buggy with a difference. A tow rope was rigged behind the buggy and the Mennonites were taking turns "skiing" from the back on a piece of cardboard!

It can strike anywhere, any time. So when I find myself lugging frozen logs from the wood pile and stripping off layers of snow-wet barn clothes while a blizzard rages outside, it does not surprise me to find my thoughts drifting into the unlikely realm of what sort of evening gown I would wear to the opera.

Wondering whether the Home Shopping Network sells Vanna White endorsed tiaras is a sure sign of the onset of cabin fever.

However, most of my symptoms manifest themselves physically.

One year I got out the stepladder and tried to clean the exterior windows in mid-winter.

Another year I bought some cement and tried sculpting a birdbath in the basement.

Last year I attempted to install new chicken wire around the old coop during a snow storm.

This year the indicators have been more subtle, but the diagnosis is definitive.

For example, I have accumulated six tins of anchovies in the pantry. I believe I must have been dreaming about summer days when the romaine is at its sweetest and a Caesar salad is called for. Or perhaps I am subconsciously stockpiling in the event of an invasion by a desalinated foreign power.

I do not even like anchovies.

I have the mail delivery timed to within five minutes, and I read every speck of it thoroughly, including the pale ink on the back of my bank statements and all flyers. On clear days I have contemplated driving 30 miles to buy a laundry hamper on sale.

I have ransacked the tour package catalogue rack at the local travel agency, and devoted myself to analyzing destinations, prices, likelihood of tornadoes and vaccination requirements.

I am not going anywhere.

I seriously thought about ordering a pair of pink pedal pushers from the Home Shopping Network. And I have considered calling one of those 900 numbers to find out what any person could possibly say that would be worth five dollars per minute.

In lieu of that, I painted my toenails shocking red.

These things, plus finding myself wandering through the barnyard gyrating wildly to old Rolling Stones tunes, led me to confirm a cabin fever diagnosis.

In my case, the cure is multi-faceted. One of these days I will leap on the bus and head for Toronto, which we up-country types call "the big smoke."

I will go to a hair stylist for a spruce up and catch up on what is "hip" by observing the shampoo person's fashion statement.

I will buy some naughty underwear and try on hats.

I will have lunch with my urban girlfriends — which will confirm for me that I could never go back to a desk job or apply that much makeup daily ever again.

On the home front, one of my favourite remedies is to take a course. So far, I have studied marine navigation, firearm safety and the art of deboning a turkey. This year I think it will be fly-fishing.

The mail is a cure in itself.

I have a drawer full of seed catalogues that started arriving before Christmas. Plans must be made and orders placed. Soon packets of giant pumpkin seeds and variegated French green beans and exotically named Chinese vegetables will arrive.

I have already set up my potting bench and gathered the old pots and trays. In a couple of weeks every window ledge will be sprouting with something and the smell of earth and growing things will make any ice storm bearable.

I don't know if city folks contract cabin fever, or if it is possible in the midst of all those buildings to notice that sundown is taking longer to come every day.

I guess cabin fever can strike anywhere.

This year my remedy for anyone who finds themselves stockpiling anchovies for no apparent reason and wearing red toe nail polish with no place to go is fairly simple.

First, order a seed catalogue. Then keep your eye open for sales on hip waders and oil your fishing reel.

Get a haircut and gyrate wildly to the Rolling Stones or whatever moves you while wearing spicy under-clothes and a new hat.

It works every time for me.

In Praise of
Long Underwear

ONE OF THE things you don't worry much about on
a farm is keeping up with current fashion. A good suit
might help when you're making your case to the bank,
but it's not going to get you very far in the barn.

Occasionally I will glance in a full-length mirror
before heading out to do my chores, and everything I
see confirms that the only fashion statement I am
making in the dead of winter is keeping warm.

In contemporary terms, you could call it Country
Grunge.

It really doesn't matter to the sheep if I look like
the Pillsbury Dough Boy in my snowsuit. The chickens
don't even blink a baleful eye at my hat with the
earflaps and the lopsided toque I wear on top. If I wear
mitts of different colours, the horses will not shun me,
and my clunky old felt-lined boots may look like something from a construction site tag sale, but they have a
lot of sole when it comes to maneuvering on ice.

of course, when you are working with animals and spending a lot of time living in their barnyard environment, you must resign yourself to the fact that at least your outer layer of clothing is bound to pick up the odours and even the evidence of animals. Somehow there is always one lone chicken roosting in the barn rafters who manages (or maybe plots) a direct plop somewhere on my toque or torso. And sheep anticipating grain are fairly direct about cuddling up to the person holding the bucket.

The horses are the same. They have no compunction about taking a great drink from their water bucket and then turning to wipe their dripping lips on me while I'm combing their tangled manes.

Outerwear takes a beating on the farm, but the backbone of any rural winter wardrobe has got to be underwear. Specifically, long underwear.

When I lived in the city, I didn't even think about owning longjohns, but in the country a woman without long underwear is nothing more than a popsicle waiting to happen. And until I got to the country I had no idea of the variety of long underwear that is available. I had a cartoon concept of a one-piece sort of uniform with a trap door in the back that never seemed quite practical for the female form.

Today there is state-of-the-art long underwear. Two-piece long underwear, colour co-ordinated long underwear, and long underwear that Madonna might consider if she ever plays Antarctica. There's combed cotton long underwear and pure wool long underwear. Long underwear printed with little snowflakes on it.

Long underwear with lace trim. Slithery, silk long underwear and denim checkered long underwear.

You've got medium-weight long underwear for cold days and expedition-weight long underwear for really cold days. On days when it's so cold that one pair of long underwear just won't do, there is puffy down-insulated long underwear to layer over top.

You can even find catalogues with huge sections devoted to long underwear. They sell underwear that "wicks" moisture away from your body, and underwear that comes with two layers so you don't have to dress yourself twice.

The most fascinating concept to date is something called the "heat strip body warmer." This appears to consist of some sort of space-age material that you wrap over your naked body, securing it with ties at the waist or wherever else you please. You plug this into a portable battery pack that you wear while the "strip" keeps you as warm as a Montserrat suntan.

Of course, you wear a layer of clothing over the heat strip lest you be mistaken for a crazed nudist, or Madonna playing Antarctica. The advertising says it's a "chill killer," but somehow I'd rather put my trust in long underwear any day — it never needs recharging.

Long underwear is like socks, you can layer them on and layer them off. You can't do that with pantyhose and bustiers. And since only you know what's really underneath, there's something simply sexy about long underwear.

I try to keep that in mind when I look in the mirror.

MAPLE MEMORIES

ONCE THERE WAS a four-storey-tall maple tree in the centre of my pasture on a high knoll overlooking the barnyard.

It was a straight and majestic tree. In the summertime the sheep would cluster at its giant base. Cows and horses would rub against its rough bark. In the spring huge flocks of crows gathered in its branches. In the fall flocks of Canada geese swept over the tops of its branches so closely that the beating of their wings would cause its gold and red leaves to flutter to the ground. In the winter its stark outline stood against the backdrop of snow, and occasionally I would find it coated in ice, glistening in the morning sun.

Two years ago the tree was struck by lightning during a brutal storm. It was night and I was alone with the dogs. The thunder clapped so loudly that the windows rattled. Forks of lightning streaked the sky. Outside, the yard was lit up like a movie set. When I saw a fork hit the ground in my garden less than 100 feet from my kitchen table, I put on my rubber boots.

Grandmother once told me she was peeling pota-toes during a lightning storm when a bolt landed outside her window and shot through the wall of the farmhouse and right across the floor to where she was standing. Lucky for her, she had just come in from the garden as the storm began and was still wearing her rubber boots. Science may disprove it, but she always claimed those rubber boats saved her life — and I always feel better if I can ride out a storm in my faithful Wellingtons.

At the peak of the storm, the hydro went out. While I was tripping over the dogs in the dark looking for matches to light the candles, a huge flash illumi-nated the barnyard.

I just caught a glimpse of the lightning as it was zapping the old maple tree. The light was unearthly — shades of purple and blue against silvery-green leaves. The ground seemed to quiver, and along with the constant thunder I could hear a great moaning creak from the tree. In the morning I discovered that the lightning had hit the tree at its crown.

All summer long the tree kept its leaves. In the autumn the leaves turned to burnished gold and only in the winter did the damage become truly apparent. Stripped of its leaves, the lightning-cracked branches were easy to see — hanging awkwardly amid the sturdy limbs.

That spring a few leaves unfurled on one side of the tree, but the rest was bare. I knew in my heart of hearts that the tree was slowly dying. A dead tree can be a dangerous thing, unstable on the ground and disquieting to all who view it. So I called John the Tree Cutter.

John emerged from his truck with a chainsaw that would have been the envy of old Leatherface, the anti-hero of the *Texas Chainsaw Massacre*. Two men anchored a rope while John sawed into the base of the big tree, taking out wedges of wood carefully to ensure that it would fall without damaging fences or lives. At one point the chain saw was silenced when a change in the wind rocked the tree backward and it sank on the saw. The men were greatly concerned about recovering their chainsaw, but I saw it as a sign of lingering character from the tree. It would not go down easy and it would go down at its own speed.

I watched the tree finally fall. I cannot remember the sound. Men were running. Suddenly there seemed to be a gaping space in the sky. John the Tree Cutter carved the tree into firewood, but I saved a big slab of it to use as a garden stool.

It hurts me to see the stump in the pasture. On summer nights the sheep still crowd around it to sleep and the lambs use it as a jumping platform in the moonlight. The horses have transferred their affections to a younger maple which I had not paid much attention to before, but it seems to be a tree with potential.

This winter, I am bidding my final farewell to the grand old maple tree. When I look for a huge and heavy hunk of wood to keep me warm all night long, I turn to the place in the woodpile where I shed a few tears while stacking its fresh-cut limbs.

The wood is dry now. Cracks splinter the great

rings where sap once flowed. At night, I fill the wood-stove with maple and sleep in comfort. In the morning, all that is left are embers.

It takes more years than I have left in this life to grow a four-storey maple tree, but it takes only a month of winter chill to reduce such singular beauty to ashes. I think that in the spring I will go back into the woods and find a suitable sapling to plant beside the weathered stump. The knoll deserves another fine tree, and perhaps one day the tree that I plant will bring as much pleasure to those who view its grandeur as my departed maple gave to me.